Other books by Marge Piercy

Poetry
BREAKING CAMP

HARD LOVING

4-TELLING (*with Bob Hershon, Emmett Jarrett, and Dick Lourie*)

TO BE OF USE

LIVING IN THE OPEN

THE TWELVE-SPOKED WHEEL FLASHING

THE MOON IS ALWAYS FEMALE

Fiction
GOING DOWN FAST

DANCE THE EAGLE TO SLEEP

SMALL CHANGES

WOMAN ON THE EDGE OF TIME

THE HIGH COST OF LIVING

VIDA

BRAIDED LIVES

Play
THE LAST WHITE CLASS (*with Ira Wood*)

Circles on the Water

CIRCLES ON THE WATER

Selected poems of

Marge Piercy

ALFRED A. KNOPF New York 1992

THIS IS A BORZOI BOOK
PUBLISHED BY ALFRED A. KNOPF, INC.

Breaking Camp was published in 1968, and *Hard Loving* in 1969 by Wesleyan University Press: thirty-eight poems are reprinted by permission of the publisher.

4-Telling was published in 1971 by The Crossing Press.

To Be of Use was published in 1973 by Doubleday & Co., Inc.

Living in the Open was published in 1976, *The Twelve-Spoked Wheel Flashing* in 1978, and *The Moon Is Always Female* in 1980 by Alfred A. Knopf, Inc.

Library of Congress Cataloging in Publication Data
Piercy, Marge.   Circles on the water.   I. Title.
PS3566.I4A6   1982   811'.54   81–17210
ISBN 0–394–52059–9   AACR2
ISBN 0–394–70779–6 (pbk.)

Manufactured in the United States of America

Published May 19, 1982
Reprinted Six Times
Eighth Printing, April 1992

Contents

From *4-TELLING*

From *TO BE OF USE*

From *LIVING IN THE OPEN*

From *THE TWELVE-SPOKED WHEEL FLASHING*

From *THE MOON IS ALWAYS FEMALE*

SEVEN NEW POEMS

Introduction

An introduction might be a kind of envoi: Go little book out into the world and wheedle your way into the lives of strangers like a stray kitten. However, a selected poems is not little; and Go big fat book out into the world and impose upon strangers like a loose elephant, lacks appeal. An introduction could be an apologia, but how redundant when the poems already coax, lecture, lull, seduce, exhort, denounce. As a poet I am bound to the attempt to capture in amber the mayflies of the moment and render them into the only jewels I have to give you. I guess I will settle for saying what I imagine I am doing.

Usually the voice of the poems is mine. Rarely do I speak through a mask or persona. The experiences, however, are not always mine, and although my major impulse to autobiography has played itself out in poems rather than novels, I have never made a distinction in working up my own experience and other people's. When I am writing, I'm not aware of the difference, to be honest. I suppose that is why I have never considered myself a confessional poet. In either case I am often pushing the experience beyond realism.

I imagine that I speak for a constituency, living and dead, and that I give utterance to energy, experience, insight, words flowing from many lives. I have always desired that my poems work for others. "To be of use" is the title of one of my favorite poems and one of my best-known books—now out of print as a result of the *Thor* decision by the IRS to tax publisher's backlists.

What I mean by being of use is not that the poems function as agitprop or are didactic, although some of them are. I have no more hesitation than Pope or Hesiod did to write in that mode as well as in many others. The notion that poetry with a conscious rather than an unconscious politics is impermissible or impure is a modern heresy of advantage only to those who like just fine the way things are going. We are social animals and we live with and off and on each other. You would have had great trouble explaining to Sophocles, Virgil, Catullus, Chaucer, Dryden, Wordsworth, Shelley, Arnold, Whitman, Blake, Goethe, that poetry refers only to other poetry and that poets are strange and special people who have no social connections, social interests, social duties.

What I mean by useful is simply that readers will find poems that speak to and for them, will take those poems into their lives and say them to each other and put them up on the bathroom wall and remember bits and pieces of them in stressful or quiet moments. That the poems may give voice to something in the experience of a life has been my intention. To find ourselves spoken for in art gives dignity to our pain, our anger, our lust, our losses. We can hear what we hope for and what we most fear, in the small release of cadenced utterance. We have few rituals that function for us in the ordinary chaos of our lives.

Although I love the work of many other poets and am always reading it and being moved by it and seeing new kinds of poems to write and new openings through the work of others, although I criticize poetry, I am not a poet who writes primarily for the approval or attention of other poets. When they like my work, I am very pleased, but poets are not my primary constituency. Poetry is too important to keep to ourselves. One of the oldest habits of our species, poetry is powerful in aligning the psyche. A poem can momentarily integrate the different kinds of knowing of our different and often warring levels of brain, from the reptilian part that recognizes rhythms and responds to them up through the mammalian centers of the emotions, from symbolic knowing as in dreams to analytical thinking, through rhythms and sound and imagery as well as overt meaning. A poem can momentarily heal not only the alienation of thought and feeling Eliot discussed, but can fuse the different kinds of knowing and for at least some instants weld mind back into body seamlessly.

Knopf has published my last three volumes of poetry. My editor, Nancy Nicholas, is extremely understanding about what I try to do with each collection. Each book is an artifact and the poems in it are placed in a particular order to work as a whole as well as individually. I may love a poem and judge it excellent and yet hold it out of book after book until at last it finds its appropriate niche. However, Nancy said to me, Establish your canon thus far with this book. That I cannot do. I have left out poems I know are favorites of readers and of critics and poems I respect as well as any here. I have merely tried to select an appropriate number of poems from each volume with some kind of balance of the various sorts I have written.

I have made minor changes in some, and a very few I have substantially altered. The minor changes are mostly an image, a line, a redundancy of which I have become aware over the years of saying these poems to audiences. Occasionally I am correcting an old typo that had corrupted the written text.

The poems I have rewritten are those, generally early ones, where I fudged. One poem, "Bronchitis on the 14th floor," I changed for publication into a monogamous poem. It was about the sense of being taken care of by three men while I was sick— the basic imagery of them as large strong animals (bears, horses pulling a troika) while I was extremely and vulnerably ill. I had always felt the poem under the printed poem, and suspected that the official version was weakened by being rendered conventionally.

With "Breaking Camp," for instance, the prevailing patriarchal mode encouraged me to write a dishonest poem. Basically it intended to be a *sursum corda* of sorts, written at a time I was becoming more and more involved in SDS and the antiwar movement and we were moving from protest to resistance. I wrote the poem with the male being the leader because that was how it was supposed to be. I was basically arguing we had to live differently and be prepared to take more risks, but I cast it as if I were giving in to my husband's insistence. Without that paraphernalia of imitation compliance, the poem is shorter, cleaner, more powerful. A kind of coyness enforced by rigid sex roles used to hurt women's work, and that poem was one of the places in my output I find it.

Except for some apprentice and overly literary work in *Breaking Camp*, and even including a fair number of poems from that, my first volume, my work is of a piece. I can do more and try more, but the voice is the same voice. If there is a change of substance, I would say it followed upon my moving from New York to Wellfleet after having lived in the center of cities my whole life. I moved because of bad health, so I could go on breathing, but the settling here had unexpected results for me.

I live here in Wellfleet in many ways like a peasant—a middle peasant—on a couple of acres where we grow all our own vegetables and some fruit and freeze, dry, pickle, can, root-cellar the surplus for the whole year. I fell in love with the land, in its fragility and fruitfulness, and I fell in love with this landscape. There is something of Michigan here that connects with early childhood visits in the car out from Detroit into heaven, whether heaven was two weeks in a rented cottage on a muddy lake with a rowboat, or Sundays at Lucy and Lon's tenant farm, where they would kill a chicken for us to take back as our big treat.

But the ocean, the salt- and fresh-water marshes, the sky and the light fascinate me too. I have sunk roots and I am really happy only when I am here. I know the city—it is bred into me, and for thirty-six years I knew nothing else summer and winter. Most of the year I spend a couple of days every week in Boston. Living in Wellfleet, I have learned a whole new language of the natural world that I am part of, and that knowledge has changed and enriched my work.

I have readers who love my poems about the Cape, about zucchini and lettuce and tomatoes, and simply skip or tune out the poems about an old working-class woman lying in a nursing home or about nuclear power. Then I have readers who love the poems they call feminist or political, but ask me why I write about blue heron and oak trees.

I have to confess, for me it is all one vision. There are occasional poems where I try to tie it all together, like "A gift of light." "The lunar cycle" does that on another, less individual, more complex level. Although I consider that cycle very, very important in the body of my work, I have included only a few of those poems here, since it forms the second half of my most recent book, *The Moon Is Always Female*.

I have included poems in this volume in a very long line, in a very short line, in a line that hovers around iambic pentameter or tetrameter, in verse paragraphs, in undifferentiated columns, in stanzas. I haven't put any rhymed poems into this collection, although once in a great while I do work in rhyme. If I rhyme, I mostly do so in the center of lines rather than on the end, where to my ear it sticks out and chimes.

Since every time I put together a collection, I leave out as much as I put in, this is very much a selection of a small piece of a number of selections. I apologize if your favorite poem is not here. Some of mine are also missing.

Marge Piercy
Wellfleet, Massachusetts
1981

From *BREAKING CAMP*

Kneeling at the pipes

Princely cockroach, inheritor,
I used to stain the kitchen wall with your brothers,
flood you right down the basin.
I squashed you underfoot, making faces.
I repent.
I am relieved to hear somebody
will survive our noises.
Thoughtlessly I judged you dirty
while dropping poisons and freeways and bombs
on the melted landscape.
I want to bribe you
to memorize certain poems.
My generation too craves posterity.
Accept this dish of well aged meat.
In the warrens of our rotting cities
where those small eggs
round as earth wait,
spread the Word.

Visiting a dead man
on a summer day

In flat America, in Chicago,
Graceland cemetery on the German North Side.
Forty feet of Corinthian candle
celebrate Pullman embedded
lonely raisin in a cake of concrete.
The Potter Palmers float
in an island parthenon.
Barons of hogfat, railroads and wheat
are postmarked with angels and lambs.

But the Getty tomb: white, snow patterned
in a triangle of trees swims dappled with leaf shadow,
sketched light arch within arch
delicate as fingernail moons.

The green doors should not be locked.
Doors of fern and flower should not be shut.
Louis Sullivan, I sit on your grave.
It is not now good weather for prophets.
Sun eddies on the steelsmoke air like sinking honey.

On the inner green door of the Getty tomb
(a thighbone's throw from your stone)
a marvel of growing, blooming, thrusting into seed:
how all living wreathe and insinuate
in the circlet of repetition that never repeats:
ever new birth never rebirth.
Each tide pool microcosm spiraling from your hand.

Sullivan, you had another five years
when your society would give you work.
Thirty years with want crackling in your hands.
Thirty after years with cities
flowering and turning grey in your beard.

All poets are unemployed nowadays.
My country marches in its sleep.
The past structures a heavy mausoleum
hiding its iron frame in masonry.
Men burn like grass
while armies grow.

Thirty years in the vast rumbling gut
of this society you stormed
to be used, screamed
no louder than any other breaking voice.
The waste of a good man
bleeds the future that's come
in Chicago, in flat America,
where the poor still bleed from the teeth,
housed in sewers and filing cabinets,
where prophets may spit into the wind
till anger sleets their eyes shut,
where this house that dances the seasons
and the braid of all living
and the joy of a man making his new good thing
is strange, irrelevant as a meteor,
in Chicago, in flat America
in this year of our burning.

Girl in white

Don't think
because her petal thighs
leap and her slight
breasts flatten
against your chest
that you warm her
alligator mind.
In August
her hand of snow
rests on your back.
Follow her through the mirror.
My wan sister.
Love is a trap
that would tear her
like a rabbit.

Noon of the sunbather

The sun struts over the asphalt world
arching his gaudy plumes till the streets smoke
and the city sweats oil under his metal feet.
A woman nude on a rooftop lifts her arms :

"Men have swarmed like ants over my thighs,
held their Sunday picnics of gripe and crumb,
the twitch and nip of all their gristle traffic.
When will my brain pitch like a burning tower?
Lion, come down! explode the city of my bones."

The god stands on the steel blue arch and listens.
Then he strides the hills of igniting air,
straight to the roof he hastens, wings outspread.
In his first breath she blackens and curls like paper.
The limp winds of noon disperse her ashes.

But the ashes dance. Each ashfleck leaps at the sun.

A valley where I don't belong

The first cocks begin clearing the throat of morning—
Who's that walking up on Pettijean mountain?—
rasping their brass cries from outflung necks
as they dig their spurs in the clammy cellar air.
Windows upon the mountain trap the first light.
Their bronze and copper plumage is emerging
from the pool of dusk. Lustily they drill the ear
with a falsetto clangor strident as mustard
raising alarm   I   I   I live   I live!

I stand with a damp wind licking my face
outside this shabby motel where a man snores
who is tiring of me so fast my throat parches
and I twist the hem of my coat thinking of it.

"The rooster, or cock, is a symbol of male sexuality,"
the instructor said, elucidating Herrick.
You stuck me with spiky elbow and matchspurt glance.
We were eighteen: we both were dancers in the woods,
you a white doe leaping with your Brooklyn satyr.
Bones and sap, I rode in the mothering earth
tasting the tough grass and my dear's salty mouth,
open and swept, in a gale of dark feathers.

We owned the poems they taught us, Leda and Europa.
We struck the earth with our heels and it pivoted,

sacred wood of blossoming crab and hanging snake,
wet smoke close to the grass and a rearing sun.

That fruit has fallen. You were burned like a Greek
just before the last solstice, but without games.
I was not there. For a long while I hadn't been.

Now you are my literary ghost.
I with broken suitcase and plump hips, about
to be expelled from this man to whom I'm bound
by the moist cord of want and the skeins of habit,
a hitchhiker in the hinterland of Ozarks.

You hardened to an edge that slashed yourself
while I have eased into flesh and accommodation.
The cry of the mouse shrill and covetous in my fingers,
I cannot keep my hands from anything.
My curiosity has been a long disaster.
I fear myself as once I feared my mother.
Still I know no more inexorable fact
than that thin red leap of bone: I live, I live.
I and my worn symbols see up the sun.

S. dead

You were unreasonably kind
three different years
and unasked defended me
in public squabble.
I praised a poem.
Gently drunk, you
gave me it.
I never saw you
again. Three
tooth yellow pages.
The fossil fern tracery
of kindness unearned
as death.

Day like a grey sponge
the car spun out in mud.
My head broke the windshield:
long streamered impact star.
When Robert pulled me out
waking I asked
who he was. Later
I pissed blood and screamed,
I rehearsed your act.

Your face is gone, and now
what will they
do with your poems?
Both poems and cars:

artifacts that move.
Loss of control smashes.
Skill looks organic.
But poems do not
 (outside of Gaelic)
kill : or save.

There's nothing
of you here,
only words moving
from anger at waste
from an itch
sorry, self seeking
from bowels and breath
entering a longer arc
than the car that killed you
toward oblivion.

Hallow Eve with spaces for ghosts

The joy of wax teeth,
to run masked through crackling bat black streets
a bag on the arm heavy with penny bars,
licorice, popcorn balls, suckers.
I knew that when I was grown out of me into glory,
doors would open every night to a reign of sugar,
into my cupped hands patter of kisses and coins.
When the last porch lights doused at the end of streets
I drifted home with stray glutted skeletons
to count over all I'd begged and for once got.

The pumpkins and pasteboard bones bore me.
I brush past tinseled children. The night
is low and noisy with a reddish neon glare
yet still a holy night ancient and silly.
My hands itch.
I light a candle and yawn, kicking the table,
but though I wait with meal and honey
no ghosts rise.

Lovers manage without ritual or the worn bits
mumbled over their hairiness damage nothing.
Birth is fat and has rooms.
But the dead sink like water into the ground.
While we are brushing our teeth a friend dies.
A month later someone tells us in a bar.
By the time we believe, everybody is embarrassed.
Then, then, we have to start wearing him out
month after month wearing down
till there's a hole where he used to be in the mind.

My nothings, grey lambs I count on my back,
shriveled sea deep babies, why can't
one night be allowed for adding postscripts,

urgent burrowing footnotes to frozen business?
Help the Poor! Utterly robbed, how could people
pray to their dead? You whom we slip over
our minds occasionally like costumes.
Don't chip off my mural. Please prune my roses.

Now it is late and cold. The wind
twiddles leaves into rattling gutter dervishes.
The last lost witch has gone home
complaining of too much popcorn, not enough love.
Put the dolls of the dead back in their box:
they do not know
you have been talking to their faces.

Landed fish

Danny dead of heart attack,
mid-forties, pretzel thin
just out of the pen for passing bad checks.
He made it as he could
and the world narrowed on him,
aluminum funnel of hot California sky.

In family my mother tells a story.
My uncle is sitting on the front steps,
it is late in the Depression,
my brother has dropped out of school.
Somehow today they got staked and the horses ran.
My uncle sits on the rickety front steps
under wisteria pale mauve and littering scent.
I climb in his lap: I say
This is my Uncle Danny, I call him Donald for short,
oh how beautiful he is,
he has green eyes like my pussycat.
A Good Humor man comes jingling and Danny carries me
to buy a green ice on a stick,
first ice burning to sweet water on the tongue
in the long Depression
with cornmeal and potatoes and beans in the house to eat.

This story is told by my mother
to show how even at four I was cunning.
Danny's eyes were milky blue-green,
sea colors I had never known.
The eyes of my cat were yellow. I was lying
but not for gain, mama. I squirm on his lap,
I am tangling my hands in his fiberglass hair.
The hook is that it pleases him

and that he is beautiful on the steps laughing
with money in the pockets of his desperate George Raft pants.
His eyes flicker like leaves,
his laugh breaks in his throat to pieces of sun.

Three years and he will be drafted and refuse to fight.
He will rot in stockade. He will swing an ax on his foot:
the total dropout who believed in his own luck.
I am still climbing into men's laps
and telling them how beautiful they are.
Green ices are still brief and wet and sweet.
Laughing, Danny leaves on the trolley with my brother.
He is feeling lucky, their luck is running
—like smelt, Danny—and is hustled clean
and comes home and will not eat boiled mush.
Late, late the wall by my bed shakes with yelling.

Fish, proud nosed conman, sea eyed tomcat:
you are salted away in the dry expensive California dirt
under a big neon sign shaped like a boomerang
that coaxes Last Chance   Stop Here   Last Chance.

A few ashes for Sunday morning

Uproot that burning tree of lightning struck veins.
Spine, wither like a paper match.

I'm telling you, this body could bake bread,
heat a house, cure rheumatic pains,
warm at least a bed.

Green wood won't catch
but I held against my belly a green stone
frog colored with remorse and oozing words
pressed to me till the night was fagged and wan.

Reek of charred hair clotting in my lungs.
My teeth are cinders,
cured my lecherous tongue.
Only me burnt, and warmed:
no one.

Concerning the mathematician

In the livingroom you are someplace else like a cat.
You go fathoms down into abstraction
where the pressure and the cold would squeeze the juice
      from my tissues.
The diving bell of your head descends.
You cut the murk and peer at luminous razorthin creatures
      who peer back,
creatures with eyes and ears sticking out of their backsides
lit up like skyscrapers or planes taking off.
You are at home, you nod, you take notes and pictures.
You surface with a matter-of-fact pout,
obscene and full of questions and shouting for supper.
You talk to me and I get the bends.
Your eyes are bright and curious as robins
and your hands and your chest where I lay my head are warm.

Postcard from the garden

I live in an orchard. Confetti of bruised petals.
Scents cascade over the gold furred bees,
over hummingbirds whose throats break light,
whose silver matings glint among the twigs.
Sun drips through those nets to puddle the grass.

If I eat from the wrong tree (whose sign I cannot
guess from bark cuneiform) my plumpness will wither,
the orchard crab and rot, the leaves blow
like cicada wings on dry winds, and dunes bury
the grey upclawing talons of choked trees.

My father was a harrier. My mother a thornbush.
My first seven years I crawled on the underside
of leaves offering at the world with soft tentative horns.

Then with lithe dun body and quick-sorting nose
I crept through a forest of snakegrass, nibbling seeds.
Before the razor shadow streaked for my hole.
With starved shanks and pumping ribs of matchstick
I squeaked my fears and scrabbling, burrowed my hopes.

Seven years a fox, meat on the wind
setting the hot nerve jangling in my throat.
Silence like dew clung to my thick brush.
The splintering lunge. Scorch of blood on my teeth.

Then a pond. Brown and brackish, alkali rimmed.
In drought a cracked net of fly-tunneled sores.
After rain, brimming and polluted by wading cattle,
sudden swarming claws and bearded larvae.

Now I live in an orchard. My breasts
are vulnerable as ripe apricots and fragrant.
To and fro my bare feet graze on the lawn,
deer sleek with plenty. My hair is loose.

These trees only intrude upon the desert.
There, in crannies and wind scraped crevices,
digging in chaparral, among rock and spine
live all the others I love except my love.

I sit on a rock on the border and call and call
in voice of cricket and coyote, of fox and mouse,
in my voice that the rocks smash back on me.
The wings of the hawk beat overhead as he hovers,
baffled but waiting, on the warm reek of my flesh.

The cats of Greece

The cats of Greece have
eyes grey as plague.
Their voices are limpid,
all hunger.
As they dodge in the gutters
their bones clack.
Dogs run from them.
In tavernas they sit
at tableside and
watch you eat.
Their moonpale cries
hurl themselves
against your full spoon.
If you touch one gently
it goes crazy.
Its eyes turn up.
It wraps itself
around your ankle
and purrs a rusty millennium,
you liar,
you tourist.

Sign

The first white hair coils in my hand,
more wire than down.
Out of the bathroom mirror it glittered at me.
I plucked it, feeling thirty creep in my joints,
and found it silver. It does not melt.

My twentieth birthday lean as glass
spring vacation I stayed in the college town
twanging misery's electric banjo offkey.
I wanted to inject love right into the veins
of my thigh and wake up visible:
to vibrate color
like the minerals in stones under black light.
My best friend went home without loaning me money.
Hunger was all of the time the taste of my mouth.

Now I am ripened and sag a little from my spine.
More than most I have been the same ragged self
in all colors of luck dripping and dry,
yet love has nested in me and gradually eaten
those sense organs I used to feel with.
I have eaten my hunger soft and my ghost grows stronger.

Gradually, I am turning to chalk,
to humus, to pages and pages of paper,
to fine silver wire like something a violin
could be strung with, or somebody garroted,
or current run through: silver truly,
this hair, shiny and purposeful as forceps
if I knew how to use it.

A married walk in a hot place

In a dusty square hemmed by pink stucco
smelling of exhaust, donkey turds and scented oil,
a tough shoves a woman loaded with sticks,
black-shawled, wizened as a dung beetle, into a wall.
He smooths his hair as he ambles.
The bus ends here. Paths go on.
In this landscape always there is someone
trying to break food from the mountains.

We came because winter had numbed us
and a torn man finally froze into the ground.
Two o'clock in hospital corridors, half
past five in the long winding halls of the body,
nights blurring, death rattled and rattled the throat
that had been his, that had been your father.
Marionette of reflexes suspended in cords
running up to bottles, down to machines,
while nurses cooed and doctors told codliver lies.
The blind eyes swerved in the swollen slots.
Legless the fish body flopped flopped
in a net of merciless functions.
We are animals the tip of a scalpel unselves.

Bulldust floats on the broken road. The brass sky
jangles. Goats' hot amber eyes of rapists watch.
No shade, but squat by this thorny blistered slope,
your face talon sharp with the habit of question,

block body and a roundness in your arms.
Predators, we met and set up housekeeping,
bedded now on rocks and potsherds and sage.

The arid heavy whoosh of a raven's flapping
chases his shadow across your pared face.
Sometimes here noon dust wisps are the dead.
On a rim a new war memorial sticks up
toothwhite. Above the joining of three defiles
totter the breached grey battlements of Phyle.
Inside among poppies we eat chicken, talking
old revolution. One standing lintel
gapes at the ravine. When the last man dies
these rocks will turn back to rock.

Only nine in the village died this winter,
the old woman said, offering nuts and sheepsmilk,
giving face of cypress, hands of olivewood,
giving kindness, myth and probably disease.
Twisted by pain I vomit. Then we grip hands
and go scrambling back over Parnes on goatpaths,
you and I, my wary love, eating our death as it eats us,
feeding each other on our living flesh
and thriving on that poison
mouthful by hot mouthful, cold breath by breath.

The Peaceable Kingdom

A painting by Edward Hicks, 1780–1849,
hung in the Brooklyn Museum

Creamcheese babies square and downy as bolsters
in nursery clothing nestle among curly lions and lowing cattle,
a wolf of scythe and ashes, a bear smiling in sleep.
The paw of a leopard with eyes of headlights
rests near calf and vanilla child.
In the background under the yellow autumn tree
Indians and settlers sign a fair treaty.
The mist of dream cools the lake.

On the first floor of the museum Indian remains
are artfully displayed. Today is August sixth, Hiroshima.
Man eats man with sauces of newsprint.
The vision of that kingdom of satisfaction
where all bellies are round with sweet grasses
blows on my face pleasantly
though I have eaten five of those animals.

All the rich flat black land,
the wide swirlmarked browngreen rivers,
leafy wheat baking tawny, corn's silky spikes,
sun bright kettles of steel and crackling wires, turn into
infinite shining weapons that scorch the earth.
The pride of our hive
packed into hoards of murderous sleek bombs.

We glitter and spark righteousness.
We are blinding as a new car in the sunshine.
Gasoline rains from our fluffy clouds.
Everywhere our evil froths polluting the waters—
in what stream on what mountain do you miss
the telltale brown sludge and rim of suds?

Peace: the word lies like a smooth turd
on the tongues of politicians ordering

the sweet flesh seared on the staring bone.
Guilt is added to the municipal water,
guilt is deposited in the marrow and teeth.
In my name they are stealing from people with nothing
their slim bodies. When did I hire these assassins?

My mild friend no longer paints mysteries of doors and mirrors.
On her walls the screams of burning children coagulate.
The mathematician with his webspangled language
of shadow and substance half spun
sits in an attic playing the flute all summer
for fear of his own brain, for fear that the baroque
arabesque of his joy will be turned to a weapon.
Three A.M. in Brooklyn: night all over my country.
Watch the smoke of guilt drift out of dreams.

When did I hire these killers? one day in anger,
in seaslime hatred at the duplicity of flesh?
Eating steak in a suave restaurant, did I give the sign?
Sweating like a melon in bed, did I murmur consent?
Did I contract it in Indiana for a teaching job?
Was it something I signed for a passport or a loan?
Now in my name blood burns like oil day and night.

This nation is founded on blood like a city on swamps
yet its dream has been beautiful and sometimes just
that now grows brutal and heavy as a burned out star.

Gasman invites the skyscrapers
to dance

Lonely skyscrapers, deserted tombs of business risen
and gone home to the suburbs for the night,
your elevators are forlorn as empty cereal boxes,
your marble paved vestibules and corridors
might as well be solid rock.
Beautiful lean shafts, nobody loves you except pigeons,
nobody is cooking cabbage or instant coffee in your high rooms,
nobody draws moustaches, nobody pisses on your walls.
Even your toilet stalls have nothing to report about the flesh.
You could be inhabited by blind white cavefish.
Only the paper lives in its metal drawers humming like bees.

The skyscrapers of the financial district dance with Gasman

The skyscrapers are dancing by the river,
they are leaping over their reflections
their lightning bright zigzag and beady reflections
jagged and shattered on East River.
With voices shrill as children's whistles they hop
while the safes pop open like corn
and the files come whizzing through the air
to snow on the streets that lie throbbing,
eels copulating in heaps.
Ticker tape hangs in garlands from the wagging streetlamps.
Standard Oil and General Foods have amalgamated
and Dupont, Schenley and AT&T lie down together.
It does not matter, don't hope, it does not matter.
In the morning the buildings stand smooth and shaven
        and straight
and all goes on whirring and ticking.
Money is reticulated and stronger than steel or stone or vision,
though sometimes at night
the skyscrapers bow and lean and leap under no moon.

Breaking camp

Now it begins:
sprays of forsythia against wet brick.
Under the paving mud seethes.
The grass is moist and tender in Central Park.
The air smells of ammonia and drains.
Cats howl their lean barbed sex.

Now we relinquish winter dreams.
In Thanksgiving snow we stood in my slum kitchen
and clasped each other and began and were afraid.
Snow swirled past the mattress on the floorboards,
snow on the bare wedding of our choice.
We drove very fast into a blizzard of fur.

Now we abandon winter hopes,
roasts and laughter of friends in a warm room,
fire and cognac, baking bread and goose on a platter,
cinnamon love in the satin feather bed,
the meshing of our neat and slippery flesh
while the snow flits like moths around the streetlamps,
while the snow's long hair brushes the pane.

I will not abandon you. I come shuddering
from the warm tangles of winter sleep
choosing you compulsively, repetitiously, dumbly as breath.
You will never subside into rest. But how
can we build a city of love on a garbage dump?
How can we feed an army on stew from barbed
wire and buttons? We browse on *The New York Times*
and die swollen as poisoned sheep.

The grey Canadian geese like arrowheads are pulled north
beating their powerful wings over the long valleys.
Soon we will be sleeping on rocks hard as axes.
Soon I will be setting up camp in gulleys, on moraine,
drinking rusty water out of my shoe.

Peace was a winter hope
with down comforters, a wall of books and tawny pears.
We are headed into the iron north of resistance.
I am curing our roast meat to leather pemmican.
We will lie in the whips of the grass under the wind's blade
fitting our bodies into emblems of stars.
We will stumble into the red morning to walk our feet raw.

The mills of injustice darken the sky with their smoke;
ash from the burning floats on every stream.
Soon we will be setting up camp on a plain of nails.
The suns of power dance on the black sky.
They are stacking the dead like bricks.

You belong to me no more than the sun that drums on my head.
I belong to nothing but my work carried like a prayer rug on
        my back.
Yet we are always traveling through each other,
fellows in the same story and the same laboring.
Our people are moving and we must choose and follow
through all the ragged cycles of build and collapse,
epicycles on our long journey guided
by the north star and the magnetic pole of conscience.

BREAKING CAMP

From *HARD LOVING*

Walking into love

1. What feeling is this?
I could not tell
if I climbed up or down.
I could feel
that the ground
was not level
and often I stumbled.
I only knew
that the light was poor,
my hands damp
and sharp fears
sang, sang like crickets
in my throat.

2. Difference of ages
As I climb above the treeline
my feet are growing numb,
blood knocks in my wrists and forehead.
Voices chitter out of gnarled bushes.
I seem to be carrying
a great many useless objects,
a saw, a globe, a dictionary,
a doll leaking stuffing,
a bouquet of knitting needles,
a basin of dried heads.
Voices sigh from calendar pages
I have lived too long to love you.
Withered and hard as a spider
I crawl among bones:
awful charnel knowledge
of failure, of death, of decay.
I am old as stone.
Who can make soup of me?
A spider-peddler with pack of self

I scrabble under a sky of shame.
Already my fingers are thin as ice.
I must scuttle under a rock
and hide in webs
of mocking voices.

3. Meditation in my favorite position

Peace, we have arrived.
The touch point
where words end
and body goes on.
That's all:
finite, all five-sensual
and never repeatable.
Know you and be known,
please you and be pleased
in act:
the antidote to shame
is nakedness together.
Words end,
body goes on
and something
small and wet and real
is exchanged.

4. A little scandal

The eyes of others
measure and condemn.
The eyes of others are watches ticking no.
My friend hates you.
Between you I turn and turn
holding my arm as if it were broken.
The air is iron shavings polarized.
Faces blink on and off.
Words are heavy.
I carry them back and forth in my skirt.
They pile up in front of the chairs.
Words are bricks that seal the doors and windows.
Words are shutters on the eyes
and lead gloves on the hands.
The air is a solid block.
We cannot move.

5. The words are said, the love is made

Sometimes your face
burns my eyes.
Sometimes your orange chest
scalds me.
I am loud and certain with strangers.
Your hands on the table
make me shy.
Your voice in the hall:
words rattle in my throat.
There is a bird in my chest
with wings too broad
with beak that rips me

..cing to get out.
I have called it
an idiot parrot.
I have called it
a ravening eagle.
But it sings.
Bird of no name
your cries are red and wet
on the iron air.
I open my mouth
to let you out
and your shining
blinds me.

6. Behold: a relationship

Suddenly I see it:
the gradual ease.
I no longer know how many times.
Afternoons blur into afternoons,
evenings melt into evenings.
Almost everyone guesses—
those who don't never will.
The alarms have stopped
except in my skin.
Tigers in a closet
we learn gentleness.
Our small habits together
are strange
as crows' tears
and easy as sofas.
Sometimes, sometimes
I can ask for what I want:
I have begun to trust you.

Community

Loving feels lonely in a violent world,
irrelevant to people burning like last year's weeds
with bellies distended, with fish throats agape
and flesh melting down to glue.
We can no longer shut out the screaming
that leaks through the ventilation system,
the small bits of bone in the processed bread,
so we are trying to make a community
warm, loose as hair but shaped like a weapon.
Caring, we must use each other to death.
Love is arthritic. Mistrust swells like a prune.
Perhaps we gather so they may dig one big cheap grave.
From the roof of the Pentagon which is our Bastille
the generals armed like Martians watch through binoculars
the campfires of draftcards and barricades on the grass.
All summer helicopters whine over the ghetto.
Casting up jetsam of charred fingers and torn constitutions
the only world breaks on the door of morning.
We have to build our city, our camp
from used razorblades and bumpers and aspirin boxes
in the shadow of the nuclear plant that kills the fish
with coke bottle lamps flickering
on the chemical night.

The neighbor

Man stomping over my bed in boots
carrying a large bronze church bell
which you occasionally drop:
gross man with iron heels
who drags coffins to and fro at four in the morning,
who hammers on scaffolding all night long,
who entertains sumo wrestlers and fat acrobats—
I pass you on the steps, we smile and nod.
Rage swells in me like gas.
Now rage too keeps me awake.

The friend

We sat across the table.
he said, cut off your hands.
they are always poking at things.
they might touch me.
I said yes.

Food grew cold on the table.
he said, burn your body.
it is not clean and smells like sex.
it rubs my mind sore.
I said yes.

I love you, I said.
That's very nice, he said
I like to be loved,
that makes me happy.
Have you cut off your hands yet?

The morning half-life blues

Girls buck the wind in the grooves toward work
in fuzzy coats promised to be warm as fur.
The shop windows snicker
flashing them hurrying over dresses they cannot afford:
you are not pretty enough, not pretty enough.

Blown with yesterday's papers through the boiled coffee morning
we dream of the stop on the subway without a name,
the door in the heart of the grove of skyscrapers,
that garden where we nestle to the teats of a furry world,
lie in mounds of peony eating grapes,
and need barter ourselves for nothing.
not by the hour, not by the pound, not by the skinful,
that party to which no one will give or sell us the key
though we have all thought briefly we found it
drunk or in bed.

Black girls with thin legs and high necks stalking like herons,
plump girls with blue legs and green eyelids and
        strawberry breasts,
swept off to be frozen in fluorescent cubes,
the vacuum of your jobs sucks your brains dry
and fills you with the ooze of melted comics.
Living is later. This is your rented death.
You grasp at hard commodities and vague lusts
to make up, to pay for each day
which opens like a can and is empty, and then another,
afternoons like dinosaur eggs stuffed with glue.

Girls of the dirty morning, ticketed and spent,
you will be less at forty than at twenty.
Your living is a waste product of somebody's mill.
I would fix you like buds to a city where people work
to make and do things necessary and good,
where work is real as bread and babies and trees in parks
where we would all blossom slowly and ripen to sound fruit.

Erasure

Falling out of love
is a rusty chain going quickly through a winch.
It hurts more than you will remember.
It costs a pint of blood turned grey
and burning out a few high paths
among the glittering synapses of the brain,
a few stars fading out at once in the galaxy,
a configuration gone
imagination called a lion or a dragon or a sunburst
that would photograph more like a blurry mouse.
When falling out of love is correcting vision
light grates on the eyes
light files the optic nerve hot and raw.
To find you have loved a coward and a fool
is to give up the lion, the dragon, the sunburst
and take away your hands covered with small festering bites
and let the mouse go in a grey blur
into the baseboard.

The cyclist

Eleven-thirty and hot.
Cotton air.
Dry hands cupped.
The shadow of an empty chandelier
swings on a refrigerator door.
In the street a voice is screaming.
Your head scurries with ants.
Anyone's arms drip with your sweat,
anyone's pliant belly
absorbs your gymnastic thrusts
as your fury subsides into butter.
You are always in combat with questionnaires.
You are always boxing headless dolls
of cherry pudding.
You are the tedious marksman in a forest of thighs,
you with tomcat's shrapnel memory
and irritable eyes.
Tenderness is a mosquito on your arm.
Your hands are calloused with careless touch.
You believe in luck and a quick leap forward
that does not move you.
You rub your sore pride into moist bodies
and pedal off, slightly displeased.

Juan's twilight dance

Nobody understood Juan.
Slight, amiable, he did not stand upon ceremony
but was unfailingly polite.
Men liked him: he deferred with wry grace
though his pride was sore and supple with constant use.
He was fascinated by mirrors and women's eyes.
When he spoke of the past he was always alone
half in shadow among shadowy forms.
No one in his stories had names. No one had faces.
He watched himself but did not listen to his voice.
Words were water or weapons.
He was always in love with the body that burned his eyes.
His need shone in the dark and the light, always new.
He could not bear suspense or indifference.
He had to be closed into love on the instant
while his need gleamed like a knife and the words spurted.
He never understood what the women minded.
He never could see how he cheated them
with words, the mercury words no one could grasp
as they gleamed and slipped and darted.
In the woman's eyes he saw himself.
He was compiling a woman he would have to love.
He was building a woman out of a hill of bodies.
The sadness of his closets: hundreds of arms,

thousands of hollow and deflated breasts,
necks and thighs smooth as new cars,
forests of hair waving and limp.
Why do they mind? They do not learn.
Time after time they grapple to win back from him
what gleamed in his face before:
the mask of desperate beautiful need
which each woman claims.
They chase each other through his hard flesh.
The bed is his mirror.
He spends into peace and indifference. He sleeps.
He is unfailingly polite, even with Donna Elvira
howling outside his door and breaking glass.
They always lose.

Learning experience

The boy sits in the classroom
in Gary, in the United States, in NATO, in SEATO
in the thing-gorged belly of the sociobeast
in fluorescent light in slowly moving time
in boredom thick and greasy as vegetable shortening.
The classroom has green boards and ivory blinds,
the desks are new and the teachers not so old.
I have come out on the train from Chicago to talk
about dangling participles. I am supposed
to teach him to think a little on demand.
The time of tomorrow's draft exam is written on the board.
The boy yawns and does not want to be in the classroom in Gary
where the furnaces that consumed his father seethe rusty smoke
and pour cascades of nerve-bright steel
while the slag goes out in little dumpcars smoking,
but even less does he want to be in Today's Action Army
in Vietnam, in the Dominican Republic, in Guatemala,
in death that hurts.
In him are lectures on small groups, Jacksonian democracy,
French irregular verbs, the names of friends
around him in the classroom in Gary in the pillshaped afternoon
where tomorrow he will try and fail his license to live.

Half past home

Morning rattles the tall spike fence.
Already the old are set out to get dirty in the sun
spread like drying coverlets around the garden
by straggly hedges smelling of tomcat.
From the steep oxblood hospital
hunched under its miser's frown of roof,
dishes mutter, pumps work, an odor
of disinfectant slops into the street
toward the greygreen quadrangles of the university.
Pickets with the facts of their poverty hoisted on sticks
turn in the street like a tattered washing.
The trustees decline to negotiate
for this is a charitable institution.

Among the houses of the poor and black nearby
a crane nods waist-high among broken bedrooms.
Already the university digs foundations
to be hallowed with the names of old trustees.
The dish and bottle washers, the orderlies march
carrying the crooked sick toward death on their backs.
The neighborhood is being cured of poverty.
Busses will carry the moppushers in and out.

Are the old dying too slowly in their garden?
Under elms spacious and dusty
as roominghouse porches the old men mutter
that they are closing the north wing,
for the land is valuable when you get down to it
and they will, down to the prairie dog bones.
This is the Home for Incurables: and the old are.
Many are the diseases that trustees are blind to,
or call incurable, like their own blindness
wide as the hoarse wind blows, mile after mile
where the city smokes sweetly as a barbecue
or sizzles like acid under nobody's sun.

Simple-song

When we are going toward someone we say
you are just like me
your thoughts are my brothers and sisters
word matches word
how easy to be together.

When we are leaving someone we say
how strange you are
we cannot communicate
we can never agree
how hard, hard and weary to be together.

We are not different nor alike
but each strange in our leather bodies
sealed in skin and reaching out clumsy hands
and loving is an act
that cannot outlive
the open hand
the open eye
the door in the chest standing open.

For Jeriann's hands

for Jeriann Hilderley

When I hug you, you are light as a grasshopper.
Your bones are ashwood the Indians used for bows.
You bend and spring back and can burn the touch,
a woman with hands that know how to pick things up.
Stiff as frozen rope words poke out
lopsided, in a fierce clothespin treble.
You move with a grace that is all function,
you move like a bow drawn taut and released.
Sometimes your wrists are transparent.
Sometimes an old buffalo man
frozen on the prairie stares from your face.
Your hair and eyes are the color of creek
running in the afternoon opaque under slanted sun.
You are stubborn and hardy as a rubber mat.
You are light as a paper airplane and as elegant
and you can fly.

The secret of moving heavy objects is balance, you said
in a grey loft full of your sculpture,
figures piercing or hung on boundaries,
leaping their thresholds, impaled on broken mirrors,
passing and gone into new space.
Objects born from you are mended, makeshift.
Their magic rides over rust and splinters and nails,
over shards of glass and cellophane beginning to rip.
Fragments of your work litter the banks of minor highways,
shattered faces of your icons lie on Hoboken junkyards,
float as smog over the East River,
grow black with the dust of abandoned coalbins.

One summer you made small rooms of wax
where people stood in taut ellipses staring and blind

with tenderness, with agony, with question and domestic terror.
They were candles burning.
You wanted to cast them in bronze but could not afford to.
The August sun melted them all.

The dancers in your plays move too in the dark
with masks and machines and chairs that trot and wail,
flimsy ragtag things that turn holy and dance
till no one is audience
but all grope and stumble in your world.
When you enter, we feel your presence burn blue,
no longer a woman, not wiry warm quick flesh
but a makeshift holy artifact
moving on the blank face of the dark as on a river:
ark, artifact, dancer of your own long breaking dance
which makes itself through you fiercely, totally passing in light
leaving you thin and darkened as burnt glass.

I am a light you could read by

A flame from each finger,
my hands are candelabra,
my hair stands in a torch.
Out of my mouth a long flame hovers.
Can't anyone see, handing me a newspaper?
Can't anyone see, stamping my book overdue?
I walk blazing along Sixth Avenue,
burning gas blue I buy subway tokens,
a bouquet of coals, I cross the bridge.
Invisible I singe strangers and pass.
Now I am on your street.
How your window flickers.
I come bringing my burning body
like an armful of tigerlilies,
like a votive lantern,
like a roomful of tassels and leopards and grapes
for you to come into,
dance in my burning
and we will flare up together like stars
and fall to sleep.

Crabs

They are light as flakes of dandruff with scrawny legs.
Like limpets they cling to the base of each curly hair,
go lurching among the underbrush for cover.
Our passions are their weathers.
Coitus is the *Santa Maria* hitting on virgin land,
an immigrant ship coming into harbor,
free homesteads for all.
Or native crabs vs. conquistadors wrestle and nip.
Or maybe they too mingle.
As the boat glides in, there they are, the native crabs
with mandolins and bouquets of bougainvillaea
swaying on the dock singing Aloha.
For three generations we haven't seen a new face.
O the boredom, the stale genes, the incest.
Or perhaps when the two shores approach
the crabs line up to leap the gap like monkeys,
the hair always lusher on the other side.
They travel as fast as gossip.
They multiply like troubles.
They cling and persist through poison and poking and picking,
dirt and soap, torrents and drought,
like love or any other stubborn itch.

Trajectory of the traveling Susan

Round Susan, somewhere Susan,
Susan with suitcase and Berlitz book and stuffed shoulderbag
flies in the air sitting down.
Your spices are waiting under the falling dust.
Strange pussies are sticking their paws under the door.
Gottlieb sits in a corner with his head loose in his hands
and plays at poking out his eyes.
The ceilings are blackboards he has scrawled with hieroglyphics.
The mailman fills up the box with nothing.

Quail Susan, pheasant Susan
riding an aluminum paperclip
between the cold stars and the jellyfish,
remember us in the broken net,
come back to us in the wooly strands of the caring web
stuck between jammed weeks and waiting testily.
Each love is singular.
The strands hang loose.

Apricot Susan, applesauce Susan
stuck up in the sky like a painted angel,
you think the web is a trap.
You see mouths open to swallow you in pieces.
You see gaping beaks and hear piercing cries of fill-me.
Susan, you are a hungry bird too with mouth wide open.
The nets we build never hold each other.
The minnow instant darts through the fingers

leaving a phosphorescent smear
and nothing else.

Jagged Susan, enamel Susan,
Susan of sullen sleeps and jabbing elbows,
of lists and frenetic starts,
of the hiss of compressed air and the doors slide shut,
you can't hang in the air like a rainbow.
We are making the revolution out of each other.
We have no place else to begin
but with our hungers and our caring and our teeth.
Each love is singular
and the community still less than the addition of its parts.
We are each other's blocks and bricks.
To build a house we must first dig a hole
and try not to fall in.

The butt of winter

The city lies grey and sopping like a dead rat
under the slow oily rain.
Between the lower east side tenements
the sky is a snotty handkerchief.
The garbage of poor living slimes the streets.
You lie on your bed and think
soon it will be hot and violent,
then it will be cold and mean.
You say you feel as empty
as a popbottle in the street.
You say you feel full of cold water
standing like an old horse trough.
The clock ticks, somewhat wrong,
the walls crack their dry knuckles.
Work is only other rooms where people cough,
only the typewriter clucking like a wrong clock.
Nobody will turn the soiled water into wine,
nobody will shout cold Lazarus alive
but you. You are your own magician.
Stretch out your hand,
stretch out your hand and look:
each finger is a snake of energy,

a gaggle of craning necks.
Each electric finger conducts the world.
Each finger is a bud's eye opening.
Each finger is a vulnerable weapon.
The sun is floating in your belly like a fish.
Light creaks in your bones.
You are sleeping with your tail in your mouth.
Unclench your hands and look.
Nothing is given us but each other.
We have nothing to give
but ourselves.
We have nothing to take but the time
that drips, drips anyhow
leaving a brown stain.
Open your eyes and your belly.
Let the sun rise into your chest and burn your throat,
stretch out your hands and tear the gauzy rain
that your world can be born from you
screaming and red.

Bronchitis on the 14th floor

The air swarms with piranhas
disguised as snow.
In the red chair my cat
licks her buttery paw.
The pear of my fever has ripened.
My clogged lungs percolate
as I simmer in sweet fat
above the flickering city.
The shocked limb of Broadway
jerks spasmodically below.
Knives flutter into ribs;
cars collapse into accordions.

My lungs shine, two lanterns.
I love the men who stand
at the foot of my bed,
whose voices tumble like bears
over the ceiling, whose hands
smell of tangerines and medicine.
Through nights of fire and grit
streaked with falling claws
they draw me golden with fever
borne safely, swiftly forward
on the galloping sleigh of my bed.

The death of the small commune

The death of the small commune
is almost accomplished.
I find it hard now to believe
in connection beyond the couple,
hard as broken bone.
Time for withdrawal and healing.
Time for lonely work
spun out of the torn gut.
Time for touching turned up earth,
for trickling seed from the palm,
thinning the shoots of green herb.
What we wanted to build
was a way station for journeying
to a new world,
but we could not agree long enough
to build the second wall,
could not love long enough
to move the heavy stone on stone,
not listen with patience
to make a good plan,
we could not agree.
Nothing remains but a shallow hole,
nothing remains
but a hole
in everything.

The track of the master builder

Pyramids of flesh sweated pyramids of stone
as slaves chiseled their stolen lives in rock
over the gilded chrysalis of dead royal grub.
The Romans built roads for marching armies
hacked like swords straight to the horizon.
Gothic cathedrals : a heaven of winter clouds
crystallizing as they rained into stone caves,
choirs of polyphonic light striking chilly slabs
where nobles with swords on and skinny saints
lay under the floor.
               Fortresses, dungeons, keeps,
moats and bulwarks. Palaces with mirrored halls ;
rooms whose views unfold into each other
like formal gardens, offer vistas and symmetry.
Skyscrapers where nobody lives filled with paper.

Where do the people live and what have they made themselves
splendid as these towers of glass, these groves of stone?
The impulse that in 1910 cast banks as temples,
where now does it build its numinous artifact?
The ziggurat, the acropolis, the palace of our dream
whose shape rings in the blood's cave like belladonna,
take form in the eagle's preyseeking soar
of the bomber, those planes expensive as cities,
the shark lean submarines of nuclear death,
the taut kinetic tower of the missile,
the dark-fiery omphalos of the all-killing bomb.

Why the soup
tastes like the *Daily News*

The great dream stinks like a whale gone aground.
Somewhere in New York Harbor
in the lee of the iron maiden
it died of pollution
and was cast up on Cape Cod by the Racepoint Light.
The vast blubber is rotting.
Scales of fat ripple on the waters
until the taste of that decay
like a sulphurous factory of chemical plenty
dyes every tongue.

Curse of the earth magician
on a metal land

Marching, a dream of wind in our chests,
a dream of thunder in our legs,
we tied up midtown Manhattan for half an hour,
the Revolutionary Contingent and Harlem,
but it did not happen
because it was not reported in any newspaper.
The riot squad was waiting at the bottom of 42nd Street
to disperse us into uncertain memory.
A buffalo said to me
I used to crop and ruminate on LaSalle Street in Chicago.
The grasses were sweet under the black tower of the Board
        of Trade.
Now I stand in the zoo next to the yaks.
Let the ghosts of those recently starved rise
and like piranhas in ten seconds flat chew down to public bones
the generals and the experts on antipersonnel weapons
and the senators and the oil men and the lobbyists
and the sleek smiling sharks who dance at the Diamond Ball.
I am the earth magician about to disappear into the ground.
This is butterfly's war song about to darken into the fire.
Put the eagle to sleep.
I see from the afternoon papers
that we have bought another country
and are cutting the natives down to built jet airstrips.
A common motif of monuments in the United States
is an eagle with wings spread, beak open
and the globe grasped in his claws.
Put the eagle to sleep.
This is butterfly's war song addressed to the Congress of Sharks.
You eat bunches of small farmers like radishes for breakfast.
You are rotting our teeth with sugar
refined from the skulls of Caribbean children. Thus far
we have only the power of earth magicians, dream and song
        and marching,

to dance the eagle to sleep.
We are about to disappear into the fire.
There is only time for a brief curse by a chorus of ghosts
of Indians murdered with smallpox and repeating rifles on
        the plains,
of Indians shot by the marines in Santo Domingo,
napalmed in the mountains of Guatemala last week.
There will be no more spring.
Your corn will sprout in rows and the leaves will lengthen
but there will be no spring running clean water through
        the bones,
no soft wind full of bees, no long prairie wind bearing feathers
        of geese.
It will be cold or hot. It will step on your necks.
A pool of oil will hang over your cities,
oil slick will scum your lakes and streams killing the trout and
        the ducklings,
concrete and plastic will seal the black earth and the red earth,
your rivers hum with radioactivity and the salmon float belly up,
and your mountains be hollowed out to hold the files of
        great corporations,
and shale oil sucked from under the Rockies till the
        continent buckles.
Look! children of the shark and the eagle
you have no more spring. You do not mind.
You turn on the sunlamp and the airconditioning
and sit at the television watching the soldiers dance.

BREAKING CAMP

HARD LOVING

From 4-TELLING

Letter to be disguised as a gas bill

Your face scrapes my sleep tonight
sharp as a broken girder.
My hands are empty shoppingbags.
Never plastered on the walls of subway night
in garish snake-lettered posters of defeat.
I was always stomping on your toes eager to stick
clippings that should have interested you into the soup.
I told and retold stories weeping mascara on your shirt.
If I introduced a girl she would sink fangs in your shin
or hang in the closet for months, a sleazy kimono.
I brought you my goathaired prickheavy men to bless
while they glowered on your chairs turning green as Swiss hats.
I asked your advice and worse, took it.
I was always hauling out the dollar watch of my pride.
Time after time you toted me home in a wheelbarrow drunk
with words sudsing, dress rumpled and randomly amorous
teasing you like an uncle made of poles to hold clotheslines up.
With my father you constantly wished I had been born
a boy or a rowboat or a nice wooden chest of drawers.
In the morning you delivered clanking chronicles of my faults.

Now you are respectable in Poughkeepsie.
Every couple of years I call you up
and your voice thickens with resentment and shame.
It is all done, it is quiet and still,
a piece of old cheese too hard to chew.

I list my own faults now ledger upon ledger
yet it's you I cannot forgive who have given me up.
Are you comfortable in Poughkeepsie with Vassar and IBM?
Do you stoke up your memory on cold mornings?
My rector, I make no more apologies,

I say my dirt and chaos are more loving
than your cleanliness and I exile no one,
this smelly hunting dog you sent to the vet's
to be put away, baby, put to sleep with all her fleas.
You murdered me out of your life.
I do not forgive, I hate it, I am not resigned.
I will howl at every hydrant for thirty years.

Sojourners

The rabbit who used to belong to Matthew
of the Parks Department now lives with Joanne.
She keeps him in an orange crate
for shitting raisins in shoes,
on bathmats, under pianos and in beds.
He is white, fat and runs like a faucet;
freed, would scuffle in closetbottoms
and with a rug for footing
do jigs, his red idiot eyes flashing.
In the crate he sulks.
His sinewy bent legs are stiff.
I am sorry for animals who scrounge their living from people
whether scavenging among ashcans and busted tenths
or tricksy and warm in kitchens:
it is hard enough for people to stand people
hard and sharp as the teeth of a saw
and at least we fuck each other.

Under the grind

Responsibilities roost on our fingers and toes
clucking and blinking.
Yes, they shall get their daily corn
the minutes of our lives scattered.
The love which I bear to you
must be scrubbed and washed and beaten on the rocks.
We will clean it
until it smells like yellow soap.
We will scrub it
until it is thin and scratchy as an old man's beard.
You are turning yourself into the Sensible Machine.
The beads of old problems rattle in your spine.
You are congealing your anger
into a hard green stone you suck and suck,
beautiful as a tiger's eye and poisonous.
You are becoming gnarled.
You are twisting like an old root inside yourself.
You will embrace nothing but paper and spines.
If you open to me, you are afraid
all your anxieties will burst free
like crows flying out of a broken safe.
Where would they fly? on whose head perch?
How would you catch them again?
No, I must keep still and mind business.
I must turn into a clock on a stick.
Look, my arms are already rough with bark.

Somehow

We need a private bush
to sprout in the clash of traffic
and deep in its thicket
we will root together.

There is a jacket on the wall.
We will leap into the pocket.
In that fuzzy hollow
our hairs will knot.

Behold the pencil sharpener
on the filing cabinet.
We will crawl through the hole,
we will bed upon shavings.

Zeus came to Danaë
in a golden shower.
I shall very carefully
wash my legs and ears.

In the form of a memorandum
you will get through.
All we need is a closet.
All we need is a big box.
All we need is a purse-
sized bed.

Missing is a pain
in everyplace
making a toothache
out of a day.
But to miss something
that never was:
the longest guilt
the regret that comes down
like a fine ash
year after year
is the shadow of what
we did not dare.
All the days that go out
like neglected cigarettes,
the days that dribble away.
How often does love strike?
We turn into ghosts
loitering outside doorways
we imagined entering.
In the lovers' room
the floor creaks,
dust sifts from the ceiling,
the golden bed has been hauled away
by the dealer
in unused dreams.

Ache's end

My sweet ache
is gone.
Sweet and painful
caramel, honey
in a broken tooth.
You were with me
like a light cold
in the bones,
a rainy day gnawing.
An awareness
that would turn down
to a faint hum
to an edging of static.
This caring
colored my life,
a wine badly fermented
with sugar and vinegar
in suspension.
A body can grow used
to a weight,
used to limping
and find it hard
to learn again
to walk straight.

BREAKING CAMP

HARD LOVING

4-TELLING

From *TO BE OF USE*

A work of artifice

The bonsai tree
in the attractive pot
could have grown eighty feet tall
on the side of a mountain
till split by lightning.
But a gardener
carefully pruned it.
It is nine inches high.
Every day as he
whittles back the branches
the gardener croons,
It is your nature
to be small and cozy,
domestic and weak;
how lucky, little tree,
to have a pot to grow in.
With living creatures
one must begin very early
to dwarf their growth:
the bound feet,
the crippled brain,
the hair in curlers,
the hands you
love to touch.

What you waited for

You called yourself a dishwater blond,
body warm and flat as beer that's been standing.
You always had to stand until your feet were sore
behind the counter
with a smile like an outsized safety pin
holding your lips off your buck teeth.

Most nights alone or alone with men
who wiped themselves in you.
Pass the damp rag over the counter again.
Tourist cabins and roadhouses of the deaf loudmouth,
ponds where old boots swim and drive-in moons.
You came to see yourself as a salesman's bad joke.
What did you ever receive for free
except a fetus you had to pay to yank out.

Troubles cured you salty as a country ham,
smoky to the taste, thick skinned and tender inside
but nobody could take nourishment
for lacking respect.
No husband, no baby, no house, nobody to own you
public as an ashtray you served
waiting for the light that came at last
straight into the windshield on the highway.

Two days later the truckers are pleased.
Your replacement is plain but ten years younger.
Women's lives are shaped like cheap coffins.
How long will she wait for change?

The secretary chant

My hips are a desk.
From my ears hang
chains of paper clips.
Rubber bands form my hair.
My breasts are wells of mimeograph ink.
My feet bear casters.
Buzz. Click.
My head is a badly organized file.
My head is a switchboard
where crossed lines crackle.
Press my fingers
and in my eyes appear
credit and debit.
Zing. Tinkle.
My navel is a reject button.
From my mouth issue canceled reams.
Swollen, heavy, rectangular
I am about to be delivered
of a baby
Xerox machine.
File me under W
because I wonce
was
a woman.

Night letter

Scalded cat,
claws, arched back and blistered pride:
my friend. You'd have cooked down
my ropy carcass in a kettle for soup.
I was honing my knife.
What is friendship
to the desperate?
Is it bigger than a meal?

Before any mirror or man we jostled.
Fought from angst to Zeno,
sucked the onion of suspicion,
poured lie on the telephone.
Always head on: one raw from divorce court
spitting toads and nail clippings,
the other fresh baked from a new final bed
with strawberry-cream-filled brain.
One cooing, while the other spat.
To the hunted
what is loyalty?
Is it deeper than an empty purse?
Wider than a borrowed bed?

Of my two best friends at school
I continued to love the first Marie better
because she died young
so I could carry her along with me,
a wizened embryo.
But you and I clawed at hardscrabble hill

willing to fight anyone
especially each other
to survive.

Couldn't we have made alliance?
We were each so sure
of the way out,
the way in.
Now they've burnt out your nerves, my lungs.
We are better fed
but no better understood,
scabby and gruff with battle.
Bits of our love are filed in dossiers
of the appropriate organizations.
Bits of our love are moldering
in the Lost and Found offices of bankrupt railroads.
Bits stick like broken glass
in the minds of our well-earned enemies.
Regret is a damp wind
off the used car lot
where most of our peers came to rest.
Now—years too late—my voice quavers,
Can I help?

In the men's room(s)

When I was young I believed in intellectual conversation:
I thought the patterns we wove on stale smoke
floated off to the heaven of ideas.
To be certified worthy of high masculine discourse
like a potato on a grater I would rub on contempt,
suck snubs, wade proudly through the brown stuff on the floor.
They were talking of integrity and existential ennui
while the women ran out for six-packs and had abortions
in the kitchen and fed the children and were auctioned off.

Eventually of course I learned how their eyes perceived me:
when I bore to them cupped in my hands a new poem to nibble,
when I brought my aerial maps of Sartre or Marx,
they said, she is trying to attract our attention,
she is offering up her breasts and thighs.
I walked on eggs, their tremulous equal:
they saw a fish peddler hawking in the street.

Now I get coarse when the abstract nouns start flashing.
I go out to the kitchen to talk cabbages and habits.
I try hard to remember to watch what people do.
Yes, keep your eyes on the hands, let the voice go buzzing.
Economy is the bone, politics is the flesh,
watch who they beat and who they eat,
watch who they relieve themselves on, watch who they own.
The rest is decoration.

The nuisance

I am an inconvenient woman.
I'd be more useful as a pencil sharpener or a cash register.
I do not love you the way I love Mother Jones or the surf
        coming in
or my pussycats or a good piece of steak.
I love the sun prickly on the black stubble of your cheek.
I love you wandering floppy making scarecrows of despair.
I love you when you are discussing changes in the class structure
and it jams my ears and burns in the tips of my fingers.

I am an inconvenient woman.
You might trade me in on a sheepdog or a llama.
You might trade me in for a yak.
They are faithful and demand only straw.
They make good overcoats.
They never call you up on the telephone.

I love you with my arms and my legs
and my brains and my cunt and my unseemly history.
I want to tell you about when I was ten and it thundered.
I want you to kiss the crosshatched remains of my burn.
I want to read you poems about drowning myself
laid like eggs without shells at fifteen under Shelley's wings.
I want you to read my old loverletters.

I want you to want me
as directly and simply and variously
as a cup of hot coffee.
To want to, to have to, to miss what can't have room to happen.
I carry my love for you
around with me like my teeth
and I am starving.

I will not be your sickness

Opening like a marigold
crop of sun and dry soil
acrid, bright, sturdy.

Spreading its cancer
through the conduits of the body,
a slow damp murder.

Breathing like the sea
glowing with foam and plankton.
Rigid as an iron post

driven between my breasts.
Will you lift your hands
and shape this love

into a thing of goodness?
Will you permit me to live
when you are not looking?

Will you let me ask questions
with my mouth open?
I will not pretend any longer

to be a wind or a mood.
Even with our eyes closed
we are walking on someone's map.

The thrifty lover

At the last moment you decided
to take the bus
rather than the plane,
to squander those hours
staring at your reflection
on a dark pane.

Then all night you rummaged
my flesh for some body else.
You pinched and kneaded
testing for ripeness, rot,
suspicious and about to reject me
or knock down the price.

You lectured me like a classroom
on your reading of the week,
used homilies, reconditioned anecdotes,
jokes with rebuilt transmissions.
All the time your eyes veered.
What's wrong, I would ask?

Nothing, you'd answer, eyes full
of nothing. He goes through women
quickly, a friend said, and now
I see how you pass through,
in a sealed train
leaving a hole like a tunnel.

A shadow play for guilt

1.

A man can lie to himself.
A man can lie with his tongue
and his brain and his gesture;
a man can lie with his life.
But the body is simple as a turtle
and straight as a dog:
the body cannot lie.

You want to take your good body off like a glove.
You want to stretch it and shrink it
as you change your abstractions.
You stand in flesh with shame.
You smell your fingers and lick your disgust
and are satisfied.
But the beaten dog of the body remembers.
Blood has ghosts too.

2.

You speak of the collective.
Then you form your decisions
and visit them on others
like an ax. Broken open I have learned
to mistrust a man whose rhetoric is good
and whose ambition is fierce:
a man who says *we*, moving us,
and means *I* and *mine*.

3.

Many people have a thing they want to protect.
Sometimes the property is wheat, oil fields, slum housing,
plains on which brown people pick green tomatoes,
stocks in safety deposit boxes, computer patents,

84

thirty dollars in a shoebox under a mattress.
Maybe it's a woman they own and her soft invisible labor.
Maybe it's images from childhood of how things should be.
The revolutionary says, we can let go.
We both used to say that a great deal.
If what we change does not change us
we are playing with blocks.

4.

Always you were dancing before the altar of guilt.
A frowning man with clenched fists
you fixed to my breasts with grappling hooks to feed
gritting your teeth for fear
a good word would slip out:
a man who came back again and again
yet made sure that his coming was attended by pain
and marked by a careful coldness,
as if gentleness were an inventory that could run low,
as if loving were an account that could be overdrawn,
as if tenderness saved drew interest.
You are a capitalist of yourself.
You hoard for fantasies and deceptions
and the slow seep of energy from the loins.
You fondle your fears and coddle them
while you urge others on.

Among your fantasies and abstractions
ranged like favorite battered toys,
you stalk with a new item, gutted
from what was alive and curious.
Now it is safe,
private and tight as a bank vault
or a tomb.

Song of the fucked duck

In using there are always two.
The manipulator dances with a partner who cons herself.
There are lies that glow so brightly we consent
to give a finger and then an arm
to let them burn.
I was dazzled by the crowd where everyone called my name.
Now I stand outside the funhouse exit, down the slide
reading my guidebook of Marx in Esperanto
and if I don't know anymore which way means forward
down is where my head is, next to my feet.
Form follows function, says the organizer
and turns himself into a paper clip,
into a vacuum cleaner,
into a machine gun.
Function follows analysis
but the forebrain
is only an owl in the tree of self.
One third of life we prowl in the grottoes of sleep
where neglected worms ripen into dragons,
where the spoiled pencil swells into an oak,
and the cows of our early sins are called home chewing their cuds
and turning the sad faces of our childhood upon us.
Come back and scrub the floor, the stain is still there,
come back with your brush and kneel down,
scrub and scrub again, it will never be clean.
Buried desires sprout like mushrooms on the chin of the morning.
The will to be totally rational
is the will to be made out of glass and steel:
and to use others as if they were glass and steel.
The cockroach knows as much as you about living.
We trust with our hands and our mouths.
The cunt accepts. The teeth and back reject.
What we have to give each other:

dumb and mysterious as water swirling.
Always in the long corridors of the psyche
doors are opening and doors are slamming shut.
We rise each day to give birth or to murder
selves that go through our hands like tiny fish.
You said : I am the organizer and took and used.
You wrapped your head in theory like yards of gauze
and touched others only as tools that fit to your task.
Arrogance is not a revolutionary virtue.
The mad bulldozers of ego level the ground.
I was a tool that screamed in the hand.
I have been loving you so long and hard and mean
and the taste of you is part of my tongue
and your face is burnt into my eyelids
and I could build you with my fingers out of dust.
Now it is over. Whether we want or not
our roots go down to strange waters,
we are creatures of the seasons and the earth.
You always had a reason and you have them still
rattling like dry leaves on a stunted tree.

A just anger

Anger shines through me.
Anger shines through me.
I am a burning bush.
My rage is a cloud of flame.
My rage is a cloud of flame
in which I walk
seeking justice
like a precipice.
How the streets
of the iron city
flicker, flicker,
and the dirty air
fumes.
Anger storms
between me and things,
transfiguring,
transfiguring.
A good anger acted upon
is beautiful as lightning
and swift with power.
A good anger swallowed,
a good anger swallowed
clots the blood
to slime.

The crippling

I used to watch it on the ledge:
a crippled bird.
How did it survive?
Surely it would die soon.
Then I saw a man
at one of the windows
fed it, a few seeds,
a crust from lunch.
Often he forgot
and it went hopping on the ledge
a starving
scurvy sparrow.
Every couple of weeks
he caught it in his hand
and clipped back one wing.
I call it a sparrow.
The plumage was sooty,
sometimes in the sun
scarlet as a tanager.
He never let it fly.
He never took it in.
Perhaps he was starving too.
Perhaps he counted every crumb.
Perhaps he hated
that anything alive
knew how to fly.

Right thinking man

The head : egg of all.
He thinks of himself as a head thinking.
He is eating a coddled egg.
He drops a few choice phrases on his wife
who cannot seem to learn after twenty years
the perfection of egg protein
neither runny nor turned to rubber.

Advancing into his study he dabbles a forefinger
in the fine dust on his desk and calls his wife
who must go twitching to reprimand
the black woman age forty-eight who cleans the apartment.
Outside a Puerto Rican in a uniform
is standing in the street to guard his door
from the riffraff who make riots on television,
in which the university that pays him owns much stock.

Right thinking is virtue, he believes,
and the clarity of the fine violin of his mind
leads him a tense intricate fugue of pleasure.
His children do not think clearly.
They snivel and whine and glower and pant
after false gods who must be blasted with sarcasm
because their barbaric heads

keep growing back in posters on bedroom walls.
His wife does not dare to think.
He married her for her breasts
and soft white belly of surrender arching up.

The greatest pain he has ever known
was getting an impacted wisdom tooth out.
The deepest suffering he ever tasted
was when he failed to get a fellowship
after he had planned his itinerary.
When he curses his dependents
Plato sits on his right hand and Aristotle on his left.
Argument is lean red meat to him.
Moses and Freud and St. Augustine are in his corner.
He is a good man and deserves to judge us all
who go making uncouth noises and bangs in the street.
He is a good man : if you don't believe me,
ask any god.
He says they all think like him.

Barbie doll

This girlchild was born as usual
and presented dolls that did pee-pee
and miniature GE stoves and irons
and wee lipsticks the color of cherry candy.
Then in the magic of puberty, a classmate said:
You have a great big nose and fat legs.

She was healthy, tested intelligent,
possessed strong arms and back,
abundant sexual drive and manual dexterity.
She went to and fro apologizing.
Everyone saw a fat nose on thick legs.

She was advised to play coy,
exhorted to come on hearty,
exercise, diet, smile and wheedle.
Her good nature wore out
like a fan belt.
So she cut off her nose and her legs
and offered them up.

In the casket displayed on satin she lay
with the undertaker's cosmetics painted on,
a turned-up putty nose,
dressed in a pink and white nightie.
Doesn't she look pretty? everyone said.
Consummation at last.
To every woman a happy ending.

Hello up there

Are you You or Me or It?
I go littering you over the furniture
and picking you out of the stew.
Often I've wished you otherwise: sleek,
docile, decorative and inert.
Yet even in daydreams I cannot imagine myself
otherwise thatched: coarse, black and abundant
like weeds burst from the slagheaps of abandoned mines.

In the '50's children used to point and shout Witch.
Later they learned to say Beatnik and later yet, Hippie,
but old grandmamas with Thessaloniki or Kiev in their throats
thought I must be nice because I looked like a peasant.
In college my mother tried to change my life
by bribing me to cut it off and have it "done."
Afterwards the hairdresser chased me waving my hair in a
            paper bag.
The next man who happened was a doctor's son
who quoted the Lord Freud in bed and on the pot,
thought I wrote poems because I lacked a penis
and beat me when he felt ugly.
I grew my hair back just as quick as I could.

Cloud of animal vibrations,
tangle of hides and dark places
you keep off the tidy and the overly clean and the wango upright.
You proclaim the sharp limits of my patience
with trying to look like somebody's wet dream.
Though I can trim you and throw you out with the coffee grounds,
when I am dead and beginning to smell worse than my shoes
presumably you will continue out of my skull
as if there were inside no brains at all
but only a huge bobbin of black wire unwinding.

High frequency

They say that trees scream
under the bulldozer's blade.
That when you give it water,
the potted coleus sings.
Vibrations quiver about leaves
our ears are too gross
to comprehend.

Yet I hear on this street
where sprinklers twirl
on exterior carpeting
a high rising whine.
The grass looks well fed.
It must come from inside
where a woman on downs is making
a creative environment
for her child.

The spring earth cracks
over sprouting seeds.
Hear that subliminal roar,
a wind through grass and skirts,
the sound of hair crackling,

the slither of anger
just surfacing.

Pressed against glass and yellowing,
scrawny, arching up to
the insufficient light, plants
that do not belong in houses
sing of what they want:

like a woman who's been told
she can't carry a tune,
like a woman afraid people will laugh
if she raises her voice,
like a woman whose veins surface
compressing a scream,
like a woman whose mouth hardens
to hold locked in her own
harsh and beautiful song.

The woman in the ordinary

The woman in the ordinary pudgy downcast girl
is crouching with eyes and muscles clenched.
Round and pebble smooth she effaces herself
under ripples of conversation and debate.
The woman in the block of ivory soap
has massive thighs that neigh,
great breasts that blare and strong arms that trumpet.
The woman of the golden fleece
laughs uproariously from the belly
inside the girl who imitates
a Christmas card virgin with glued hands,
who fishes for herself in other's eyes,
who stoops and creeps to make herself smaller.
In her bottled up is a woman peppery as curry,
a yam of a woman of butter and brass,
compounded of acid and sweet like a pineapple,
like a handgrenade set to explode,
like goldenrod ready to bloom.

Unlearning to not speak

Blizzards of paper
in slow motion
sift through her.
In nightmares she suddenly recalls
a class she signed up for
but forgot to attend.
Now it is too late.
Now it is time for finals:
losers will be shot.
Phrases of men who lectured her
drift and rustle in piles:
Why don't you speak up?
Why are you shouting?
You have the wrong answer,
wrong line, wrong face.
They tell her she is womb-man,
babymachine, mirror image, toy,
earth mother and penis-poor,
a dish of synthetic strawberry icecream
rapidly melting.
She grunts to a halt.
She must learn again to speak
starting with I
starting with We
starting as the infant does
with her own true hunger
and pleasure
and rage.

Women's laughter

1.

When did I first become aware—
hearing myself on the radio?
listening to tapes of women in groups?—
of that diffident laugh that punctuates,
that giggle that apologizes,
that bows fixing parentheses before, after.
That little laugh sticking
in the throat like a chicken bone.

That perfunctory dry laugh
carries no mirth, no joy
but makes a low curtsy, a kowtow
imploring with praying hands:
forgive me, for I do not
take myself seriously.
Do not squash me.

2.

My friend, on the deck we sit
telling horror stories
from the *Marvel Comics* of our lives.
We exchange agonies, battles and after each
we laugh madly and embrace.

That raucous female laughter
is drummed from the belly.
It rackets about kitchens,
flapping crows
up from a carcass.
Hot in the mouth as horseradish,
it clears the sinuses
and the brain.

3.

Years ago I had a friend
who used to laugh with me
braying defiance, as we roar
with bared teeth.
After the locked ward
where they dimmed her with drugs
and exploded her synapses,
she has now that cough
fluttering in her throat
like a crippled pigeon
as she says, but of course
I was sick, you know,
and laughs blood.

Burying blues for Janis

Your voice always whacked me right on the funny bone
of the great-hearted suffering bitch fantasy
that ruled me like a huge copper moon with its phases
until I could, partially, break free.
How could I help but cherish you for my bad dreams?
Your voice would grate right on the marrow-filled bone
that cooks up that rich stew of masochism where we swim,
that woman is born to suffer, mistreated and cheated.
We are trained to that hothouse of ripe pain.
Never do we feel so alive, so in character
as when we're walking the floor with the all-night blues.
When some man not being there who's better gone
becomes a lack that swells up to a gaseous balloon
and flattens from us all thinking and sensing and purpose.

Oh, the downtrodden juicy longdrawn female blues:
you throbbed up there with your face slightly swollen
and your barbed hair flying energized and poured it out,
the blast of a furnace of which the whole life is the fuel.
You embodied that good done-in mama who gives and gives
like a fountain of boozy chicken soup to a rat race of men.
You embodied the pain hugged to the breasts like a baby.
You embodied the beautiful blowzy gum of passivity,
woman on her back to the world endlessly hopelessly raggedly
offering a brave front to be fucked.
That willingness to hang on the meathook and call it love,
that need for loving like a screaming hollow in the soul,
that's the drug that hangs us and drags us down
deadly as the icy sleet of skag that froze your blood.

The best defense is offensive

The turkey vulture,
a shy bird ungainly on the ground
but massively graceful in flight,
responds to attack
uniquely.
Men have contempt for this scavenger
because he eats without killing.
When an enemy attacks,
the turkey vulture vomits:
the shock and disgust of the predator
are usually sufficient
to effect his escape.
He loses only his dinner,
easily replaced.
All day I have been thinking
how to adapt
this method of resistance.
Sometimes only the stark
will to disgust
prevents our being consumed:
there are clearly times
when we must make a stink
to survive.

Icon

In the chapel where I could praise
that is just being built,
the light bleeding through one window blazons
a profiled centaur whose colors mellow the sun.

See her there: hoofs braced into the loam,
banner tail streaming, burnished thighs,
back with the sheen of china but sturdy as brick,
that back nobody rides on.
Instead of a saddle, the poised arms,
the wide apart breasts, the alert head
are thrust up from the horse's supple torso
like a swimmer who breaks water to look
but doesn't clamber out or drown.

She is not monstrous
but whole in her power, galloping:
both the body tacking to the seasons of her needs
and the tiger lily head aloft with tenacious gaze.
This torso is not ridden.
This face is no rider.
As a cascade is the quickening of a river,
here thought shoots in a fountain to the head
and then slides back through
those rippling flanks again.

Some collisions bring luck

I had grown invisible as a city sparrow.
My breasts had turned into watches.
Even my dreams were of function and meeting.

Maybe it was the October sun.
The streets simmered like laboratory beakers.
You took my hand, a pumpkin afternoon
with bright rind carved in a knowing grin.
We ran upstairs.
You touched me and I flew open.
Orange and indigo feathers broke through my skin.
I rolled in your coarse rag-doll hair.
I sucked you like a ripe apricot down to the pit.
Sitting crosslegged on the bed we chattered
basting our lives together with ragged stitches.

Of course it all came apart
but my arms glow with the fizz of that cider sun.
My dreams are of mating leopards and bronze waves.
We coalesced in the false chemistry of words
rather than truly touching
yet I burn cool glinting in the sun
and my energy sings like a teakettle all day long.

We become new

How it feels to be touching
you : an Io moth, orange
and yellow as pollen,
wings through the night
miles to mate,
could crumble in the hand.

Yet our meaning together
is hardy as an onion
and layered.
Goes into the blood like garlic.
Sour as rose hips,
gritty as whole grain,

fragrant as thyme honey.
When I am turning slowly
in the woven hammocks of our talk,
when I am chocolate melting into you,
I taste everything new
in your mouth.

You are not my old friend.
How did I used to sit
and look at you ? Now
though I seem to be standing still
I am flying flying flying
in the trees of your eyes.

Meetings like hungry beaks

There is only time to say the first word,
there is only time to stammer the second.
Traffic jams the highways of nerve,
lungs fill with the plaster of demolition.
Each hour has sixty red and gold and black hands
welding and plucking and burning.

Your hair crosses my mouth in smoke.
The bridge of arms,
the arch of backs:
our fingers clutch.
The violet sky lights and crackles
and fades out.

I am at a desk adding columns of figures.
I am in a supermarket eyeing meat.
The scene repeats on the back of my lids
like an advertisement in neon
for another world.

To be of use

The people I love the best
jump into work head first
without dallying in the shallows
and swim off with sure strokes almost out of sight.
They seem to become natives of that element,
the black sleek heads of seals
bouncing like half-submerged balls.

I love people who harness themselves, an ox to a heavy cart,
who pull like water buffalo, with massive patience,
who strain in the mud and the muck to move things forward,
who do what has to be done, again and again.

I want to be with people who submerge
in the task, who go into the fields to harvest
and work in a row and pass the bags along,
who are not parlor generals and field deserters
but move in a common rhythm
when the food must come in or the fire be put out.

The work of the world is common as mud.
Botched, it smears the hands, crumbles to dust.
But the thing worth doing well done
has a shape that satisfies, clean and evident.
Greek amphoras for wine or oil,
Hopi vases that held corn, are put in museums
but you know they were made to be used.
The pitcher cries for water to carry
and a person for work that is real.

Bridging

Being together is knowing
even if what we know
is that we cannot really be together
caught in the teeth of the machinery
of the wrong moments of our lives.

A clear umbilicus
goes out invisibly between,
thread we spin fluid and finer than hair
but strong enough to hang a bridge on.

That bridge will be there
a blacklight rainbow arching out of your skull
whenever you need
whenever you can open your eyes and want
to walk upon it.

Nobody can live on a bridge
or plant potatoes
but it is fine for comings and goings,
meetings, partings and long views
and a real connection to someplace else
where you may
in the crazy weathers of struggle
now and again want to be.

Doing it differently

1.

Trying to enter each other,
trying to interpenetrate and let go.
Trying not to lie down in the same old rutted bed
part rack, part cocoon.
We are bagged in habit
like clothes back from the cleaners.
The map of your veins has been studied,
your thighs have been read and reported,
a leaden mistrust of the rhetoric of tenderness
thickens your tongue.
At the worst you see old movies in my eyes.
How can I persuade you that every day we choose
to give birth, to murder or feed our friends, to die a little.

2.

You are an opening in me.
Smoke thick as pitch blows in,
a wind bearing ribbons of sweet rain,
and the sun as field of dandelions, as rusty razor blade.
Scent colors the air with tear gas, with lemon lilies.
Most of the time you are not here.
Mostly I do not touch you.
Mostly I am talking to someone else.

I crawl into you, a bee furry with greed
into the deep trumpeting throat of a crimson lily
speckled like a newly hatched robin.
I roll, heavy with nectar.
Later, I will turn this afternoon into honey
and live on it, frugally.
It will sweeten my tea.

3.

In the pit of the night our bodies merge,
dark clouds passing through each other in lightning,
the joining of rivers far underground in the stone.
I feel thick but hollow, a polyp floating on currents.
My nerves have opened wide mouths
to drink you in and sing O O on the dark
till I cannot fix boundaries where you start and I stop.
Then you are most vulnerable.
In me that nakedness does not close by day.
My quick, wound, door, my opening,
my lidless eye.

Don't you think it takes trust,
your strength, your temper always
in the room with us like a doberman leashed.

Touch is the primal sense—
for in the womb we swam lapped and tingling.
Fainting, practicing death, we lose
sight first, then hearing, the mouth and nose deaden
but still till the end we can touch.
I fear manipulation by that handle.

Trust flourishes like a potato plant, mostly underground:
wan flowers, dusty leaves chewed by beetles,
but under the mulch as we dig
at every node of the matted tangle
the tubers, egg-shaped and golden with translucent skin,
tumble from the dirt to feed us
homely and nourishing.

4.

The Digger Indians were too primitive,
pushed onto the sparse alkaline plateau,
to make pottery that could stand on the fire.
They used to make soup by heating an oval stone
and dropping it in the pot cracking hot.
When traders came and sold them iron kettles
the women found cooking easier
but said the soup never tasted so good again.

Soup stone
blunt, heavy in my hands,
you soak, you hold, you radiate warmth,
you can serve as a weapon,
you can be used again and again
and you give a flavor to things I could miss.

5.

Beds that are mirrors,
beds that are rotisseries where I am the barbecue,
beds that are athletic fields for the Olympic trials,
beds that are dartboards, beds that are dentist's chairs,
beds that are consolation prizes floating on chicken soup,
beds where lobotomies are haphazardly performed, beds
that ride glittering through lies like a ferris wheel,
all the beds where a woman and a man
try to steal each other's bones
and call it love.

Yet that small commitment floating on a sea of spilled blood
has meaning if we inflict it.
Otherwise we fail into dry accommodation.
If we do not build a new loving out of our rubble

we will fall into a bamboo-staked trap on a lush trail.
You will secrete love out of old semen and gum and dreams.
What we do not remake
plays nostalgic songs on the jukebox of our guts,
and leads us into the old comfortable temptation.

6.

You lay in bed depressed, passive as butter.
I brought you a rose I had grown. You said
the rose was me, dark red and perfumed and three-quarters open,
soft as sometimes with embarrassment you praise my skin.
You talked of fucking the rose. Then you grew awkward;
we would never be free of roles, dominance and submission,
we slam through the maze of that pinball machine forever.

I say the rose is a place where we make love.
I am a body beautiful only when fitted with yours.
Otherwise, it walks, it lifts packages, it spades.
It is functional or sick, tired or sturdy. It serves.
Together we are the rose, full, red as the inside
of the womb and head of the penis,
blossoming as we encircle, we make that symmetrical
        fragrant emblem,
then separate into discrete workday selves.
The morning mail is true. Tomorrow's picketline is true.
And the rose, the rose of our loving
crimson and sonorous as a cellist
bowing on the curve of our spines, is true.

7.

We will be equal, we say, new man and new woman.
But what man am I equal to before the law of court or custom?
The state owns my womb and hangs a man's name on me

like the tags hung on dogs, my name is, property of.
The language betrays us and rots in the mouth
with its aftertaste of monastic sewers on the palate.
Even the pronouns tear my tongue with their metal plates.

You could strangle me: my hands
can't even encircle your neck.
Because I open my mouth wide and stand up roaring
I am the outlawed enemy of men.
A party means what a bullfight does to the bull.
The street is a gauntlet.
I open my mail with tongs.
All the images of strength in you, fathers and prophets
        and heroes,
pull against me, till what feels right to you
wrongs me, and there is no rest from struggle.

We are equal if we make ourselves so, every day, every night
constantly renewing what the street destroys.
We are equal only if you open too on your heavy hinges
and let your love come freely, freely, where it will never be safe,
where you can never possess.

8.

When we mesh badly, with scraping and squeaking,
remember that every son had a mother
whose beloved son he was,
and every woman had a mother
whose beloved son she wasn't.
What feels natural and easy is soft murder
of each other and that mutant future
striving to break into bloom
bloody and red as the real rose.

Periodic, earthy, of a violent tenderness
it is the nature of this joining
to remain partial and episodic
yet feel total: a mountain that opens like a door
and then closes
like a mountain.

The spring offensive of the snail

Living someplace else is wrong
in Jerusalem the golden
floating over New England smog,
above paper company forests,
deserted brick textile mills
square brooders on the rotten rivers,
developer-chewed mountains.

Living out of time is wrong.
The future drained us thin as paper.
We were tools scraping.
After the revolution
we would be good, love one another
and bake fruitcakes.
In the meantime eat your ulcer.

Living upside down is wrong,
roots in the air
mouths filled with sand.
Only what might be sang.
I cannot live crackling
with electric rage always.
The journey is too long
to run, cursing those
who can't keep up.

Give me your hand.
Talk quietly to everyone you meet.
It is going on.
We are moving again
with our houses on our backs.
This time we have to remember
to sing and make soup.
Pack the *Kapital* and the vitamin E,
the basil plant for the sill,

114

Apache tears you
picked up in the desert.

But remember to bury
all old quarrels
behind the garage for compost.
Forgive who insulted you.
Forgive yourself for being wrong.
You will do it again
for nothing living
resembles a straight line,
certainly not this journey
to and fro, zigzagging
you there and me here
making our own road onward
as the snail does.

Yes, for some time we might contemplate
not the tiger, not the eagle or grizzly
but the snail who always remembers
that wherever you find yourself eating
is home, the center
where you must make your love,
and wherever you wake up
is here, the right place to be
where we start again.

Councils

(for two voices, female and male)

♀   We must sit down
and reason together.
We must sit down.
Men standing want to hold forth.
They rain down upon faces lifted.

♂   We must sit down on the floor
on the earth
on stones and mats and blankets.
There must be no front to the speaking
no platform, no rostrum,
no stage or table.
We will not crane
to see who is speaking.

♀   Perhaps we should sit in the dark.
In the dark we could utter our feelings.
In the dark we could propose
and describe and suggest.

♂   In the dark we could not see who speaks
and only the words
would say what they say.

♀   Thus saying what we feel and what we want,
what we fear for ourselves and each other
into the dark, perhaps we could begin
to begin to listen.

♂ Perhaps we should talk in groups
    small enough for everyone to speak.

♀ Perhaps we should start by speaking softly.
    The women must learn to dare to speak.

♂ The men must bother to listen.

♀ The women must learn to say, I think this is so.

♂ The men must learn to stop dancing solos on the ceiling.
    After each speaks, she or he
    will repeat a ritual phrase:

♀&♂ It is not I who speaks but the wind.
    Wind blows through me.
    Long after me, is the wind.

Laying down the tower

Each of the following poems issues from a card in the Tarot deck. The Tarot cards have existed in some form since the Renaissance, and always they have carried a heretical meaning in their rich freight of the common symbols of Western culture, Western literature. I first ran across them many, many years ago when I was passionately involved in Yeats, his poetry, his ideas, the people whose work touched his own, including the creators of the deck I use still, Pamela Colman Smith and Arthur Edward Waite.

In the late sixties I began to handle the cards again. Whether using them in a mixture of divination and covert advice-giving to friends or meditating on individual cards, I found they stirred my imagination and often provided imagery that would enter my work. For me they are rich and disturbing and provoke many levels of responding, feeling and knowing.

These eleven poems are the cards of a Tarot reading. As in any reading, the context of the total set influences the way individual cards are interpreted. Every reading of the cards implies judgments—a valuing of some attributes and activities and a condemning of others. Every reading has underlying it a clumping of ideas about self and others, about good and bad, about female and male, about what winning and losing mean.

This reading is political; the values are different from the more conventional ways of reading the deck. But they're not any more present than in the ways that say the Nine of Cups is a fortunate card because it means you get a lot of "goods" to have and hold.

We must break through the old roles to encounter our own meanings in the symbols we experience in dreams, in songs, in vision, in meditation. Some of these symbols are much older than capitalism, and some contain knowledge we must recover; but we receive all through a filter that has aligned the stuff of our dreams, our visions, our poetry by values not our own.

What we use we must remake. Then only we are not playing with dead dreams but seeing ourselves more clearly, and more clearly becoming. The defeated in history lose their names, their goddesses, their language, their culture. The myths we imagine we are living (old westerns, true romances) shape our choices.

Some of the most significant myths are those of history. Here I am reconciling myself to my own history and trying to bring my sense of that history to you. I experience current media and official formulas about the recent past as an assault, a robbery. At the same time, in my third movement I go through a sense of ghostly recurrence, of centrifugal forces and schisms that unnecessarily rack and divide. Each succeeding movement has been for me a qualitative change in depth of personal involvement, in perception of the world, in what I want; the totality of the struggle in the women's movement has shaken me and altered me past the level of conscious mind. But trying to write our own history is of common concern, for if we cannot learn from that recent past and each other, we become our worst rhetoric. Whatever is not an energy source is an energy sink.

1973

The queen of pentacles

This is my deck I unwrap, and this is the card for me.
I will in any house find quickly like my sister the cat
the most comfortable chair, snug out of drafts.
Empathy flows through my fingers : I need to touch.
I am at home in that landscape of unkempt garden,
mulch and manure, thorny blackberry and sunflower and
       grape coiling,
tomato plants mad with fecundity bending their stakes,
asparagus waving fronds in the wind.

Even in a New York apartment with dirt
bought in bags like chocolate candy, I raised herbs.
I prefer species roses rough as weeds
with a strong scent, simple flowers and hips good for jam.
I like wine's fine weather on my palate.
I can sink into my body like a mole
and be lost in the tunnels of the nerves, suckling.
I want to push roots deep in my hillside and sag with ripeness,
an apple tree sprawling with fruit.

The music sacred to me speaks through drums
directly on my pulses, into the chambers of my brain.
Yet this knowing is hard and bloody, that should dance
       through us.
Too many have been murdered from the sky,
the soil has been tainted and blows away and the water stinks.

I want to grow into the benign mother with open hands
healing and fertile but must spay myself to serve,

sear off one breast like an Amazon to fight
for even the apple that shines in the hand
is secretly waxed and full of poison.
The orange is dyed with the blood of the picker.
The peach plucked green tastes of paper dollars,
run off by the emperor to finance his wars.

How often my own words set my teeth on edge
sour and hard, tearing the roof of my mouth.
What I do well and what I must do make war in my chest.
Through other women sometimes I can touch
pruned selves, smothered wishes, small wet cries that vanished
and think how all together we make up one good strong woman.
Still to get strength
for the things we have to do that frighten me
I go and dig my hands into the ground.

The tower struck by lightning reversed; the overturning of the tower

All my life I have been a prisoner under the Tower.
Some say that grey lid is the sky. Our streets are hammers.
Grey is the water we drink, grey the face I cannot love in
    the mirror,
grey is the money we lack, the itch and scratch of skins rubbing.
Grey is the color of work without purpose or end,
and the cancer of hopelessness creeping through the gut.
In my bones are calcium rings of the body's hunger
from grey bread that turns to ash in the belly.
In my brain schooled lies rot into self-hatred: and who
can I hate in the cattle car subway
like the neighbor whose elbow cracks my ribs?

The Tower of Baffle speaks bureaucratic and psychologese,
multiple choice, one in vain, one insane, one trite as rain.
Military bumblewords, pre-emptive stroke, mind and body count
    and strategic omelet.
Above in the sun live those who own, making our weather with
    their refuse.
Their neon signs instruct us through the permanent smog.
Rockefellers, Mellons and Du Ponts, you Fords and Houghtons,
who are you to own my eyes? Who gave me to be your serf?
I have never seen your faces but your walls surround me.
With the loot of the world you built these stinking cities
    as monuments.
The Tower is ugly as General Motors, as public housing,
as the twin piles of the World Trade Center,

tallest, biggest and menacing as fins on an automobile,
horns on a Minotaur programmed to kill.

The weight of the Tower is in me. Can I ever straighten?
You trained me in passivity to lay for you like a doped hen.
You bounce your gabble off the sky to pierce our brains.
Your loudspeakers from every television and classroom
and your transistors grafted onto my nerves at birth
shout you are impregnable and righteous forever.
But any structure can be overthrown.

London Bridge with the woman built into the base
as sacrifice is coming down.
The Tower will fall if we pull together.
Then the Tower reversed, symbol of tyranny and oppression,
shall not be set upright.
We are not turning things over merely
but we will lay the Tower on its side.
We will make it a communal longhouse.

The nine of cups

Not fat, not gross, just well fed and hefty he sits before
    what's his,
the owner, the ultimate consumer, the overlord.
No human kidneys can pump nine cups of wine through
but that's missing the point of having: possession is power
whether he owns apartment houses or herds of prime beef
or women's soft hands or the phone lines or the right to kill
or pieces of paper that channel men's working hours.

He is not malcontent. He has that huge high-colored
healthy face you see on executives just massaged.
He eats lobster, he drinks aged scotch, he buys pretty women.
He buys men who write about how he is a servant
    of circumstance.
He buys armies to shoot peasants squatting on his oil.

He is your landlord: he shuts off the heat and the light and
    the water,
he shuts off air, he shuts off growth, he shuts off your sex.
He buys men who know geology for him, he buys men who
    count stars,
he buys women who paint their best dreams all over his ceiling.
He buys giants who grow for him and dwarfs who shrink
and he eats them all, he eats, he eats well,
he eats and twenty Bolivians starve, a division of labor.

You are in his cup, you float like an icecube, you sink like
    an onion.
Guilt is the training of his servants that we may serve harder.
His priests sell us penance for his guilt,

his psychiatrists whip our parents through our cold bowels,
his explainers drone of human nature and the human condition.

He is squatting on our heads laughing. He belches with health.
He feels so very good he rewards us with TV sets
which depict each one of us his servants sitting
just as fat and proud and ready to stomp
in front of the pile of tin cans we call our castle.

On the six o'clock news the Enemy attacks.
Then our landlord spares no expense to defend us,
for the hungry out there want to steal our TV sets.
He raises our taxes one hundred per cent
and sells us weapons and sends us out to fight.
We fight and we die, for god, country and the dollar
and then we come back home
and he raises the rent.

The knight of swords

I was a weapon. I brandished myself, I was used in the air.
We rushed in waves at the Tower and were hurtled back.
Because we were right, should we not win?

When you know that in the foreign and domestic colonies
people are dying of hunger, of napalm, of gas, of rats, of racism,
dying and dying each death is a drop of blood falling
all night on your forehead, each death is a nail tapped in.
It is participation in murder
to sit one moment longer at the key punch.
It is guilt by association to raise your hand in class.
It is being an accomplice to take a job in the lab.
Buying a car, you pay for a fragmentation bomb.

If you are not fighting, are you not supporting?
If you saw the children starving in Brazil, would you wait
the five minutes that is five more bodies bloating?
If you saw the children burning in the bombed villages of Laos
would you have another coffee and eat the jelly doughnut?
If you saw the inside of that prison, would you switch channels?

So run at the barricade and throw back the canister of gas.
So take the club in your face and keep on slugging.
We must win, we must win for everybody so we cannot,
we can never pause, we have no time to look, we cannot breathe.

Run, keep running, don't look sideways.
The blood is raining down all the time, how can we rest?
How can we pause to think, how can we argue with you,
how can we pause to reason and win you over?
Conscience is the sword we wield,
conscience is the sword that runs us through.

The eight of swords

Bound, blinded, stymied, with bared blades for walls
and alone, my eyes and mouth filled up with dark.
We had grown used to a Movement, that sense of thaw,
things breaking loose and openings and doors pushed by the wind,
spring after the end of the Age of Ice.
Used to feeling connected, used to sisters and brothers,
used to an us that felt bigger and warmer than them.

We grew like weeds in sand.
We lusted after brave loud crashing rhetoric
and threw small gains away because they made no show.
We clashed on each other, we chopped, we never hit harder
than when we were axing a comrade two feet to the right.
Factions charred our energies. Repression ground us.

Some they bought off, some they shot down,
some they locked in their prisons or their asylums,
some they wasted with their heroin pumped in the streets,
some they have broken in hospitals, some they have gagged,
some they tormented till we rushed into death screaming rage,
some they tricked into despair so we stood impaled:
no longer could we imagine winning.

Despair is the worst betrayal, the coldest seduction:
to believe at last that the enemy will prevail.
Hush, the heart's drum, my life, my breath.
There is finally a bone in the heart that does not break
when we remember we are still part of each other,
the muscle of hope that goes on in the dark
pumping the blood that feeds us.

The seven of pentacles

Under a sky the color of pea soup
she is looking at her work growing away there
actively, thickly like grapevines or pole beans
as things grow in the real world, slowly enough.
If you tend them properly, if you mulch, if you water,
if you provide birds that eat insects a home and winter food,
if the sun shines and you pick off caterpillars,
if the praying mantis comes and the ladybugs and the bees,
then the plants flourish, but at their own internal clock.

Connections are made slowly, sometimes they grow underground.
You cannot tell always by looking what is happening.
More than half a tree is spread out in the soil under your feet.
Penetrate quietly as the earthworm that blows no trumpet.
Fight persistently as the creeper that brings down the tree.
Spread like the squash plant that overruns the garden.
Gnaw in the dark and use the sun to make sugar.

Weave real connections, create real nodes, build real houses.
Live a life you can endure: make love that is loving.
Keep tangling and interweaving and taking more in,
a thicket and bramble wilderness to the outside but to us
interconnected with rabbit runs and burrows and lairs.

Live as if you liked yourself, and it may happen:
reach out, keep reaching out, keep bringing in.
This is how we are going to live for a long time: not always,
for every gardener knows that after the digging, after
        the planting,
after the long season of tending and growth, the harvest comes.

The magician

Fusion is miracle and there is no other way, it is necessary.
Every new age is unbelievable beforehand and after, inevitable.
History is a game played backwards only.

I fling my eyes into the maw of the sun.
With all our strength, we thrust into fierce light.
We are yearning like frogs bulging our throats in the
          spring marsh
and croaking harsh and ridiculous spasms of hope.
I tell you, roses want to bloom out of the wood,
the goodness in people wants to break free
of the blind ego.
Birth is a miracle in every germinating seed.

We had thought we were waiting our Messiah, our Lenin,
our golden Organizer who would fuse us into one body
but now we see when we grow heads they lop them off.
We must be every one the connection between energy and mass,
every one the lightning that strikes to topple the tower.
Each must conduct light, heat and crackling strength
into each other: we must open a thousand fiery eyes and mouths
of flame that make us visible and pass to others.

The lion arches in my back, the goat kicks in my legs.
You skim, a glinting dragonfly, into my head and we couple in air.
Each time we say *sisters*,
each time you say *brothers*, we are making magic

for we were born each to scream alone, a worm in armor,
trained to grab at all and cherish nothing.

Every soul must become a magician; the magician is in touch.
The magician connects. The magician helps each thing
to open into what it truly wants to utter.
The saying is not the magic: we have drunk words and eaten
manifestoes and grown bloated on resolutions
and farted winds of sour words that left us weak.
It is in the acting with the strength we cannot
really have till we have won.

Give birth to me, sisters, in struggle we transform
ourselves, but how often, how often
we need help to cut loose, to cry out, to breathe!
In the skull, floating on drugs, everybody is born again good
but how hard to make that miracle pass in the streets.
This morning we must make each other strong.
Change is qualitative: we are
each other's miracle.

The three of cups

A poem is a dancing: it goes out of a mouth to your ears
and for some moments aligns us,
so we wheel and turn together.
The blackbirds dance over the marsh as they drive off the hawk.
The marsh hawks hunt in spirals paired, crying.
The bees dance where the pollen is to be gathered, and dance
            their fierce mating.

When I dance I forget myself, I am danced.
Music fills me to overflowing and the power moves
up from my feet to my fingers, making leaves as sap does.

My dance is of you: we are dancing together though scattered,
atomistic as Brownian motes, the same music holds us.
Even after Altamont, even after we have discovered
we are still death's darling children, born of the print-out,
the laser, the war-game, the fragmentation weapons of education,
still we must bear joy back into the world.
We must rise up in joy and endurance,
we must shake off the oil of passivity and no more be spectators
even before the masque of our own dark and bright dreams.

We grew up in Disneyland with ads for friends
and believed we could be made new by taking a pill.
We wanted instant revolution, where all we had to add
was a little smoke.
There is no tribe who dance and then sit down
and wait for the crops to harvest themselves
and supper to roll over before the pot.
We shall survive only if we win; they will kill us
if they can, and killing is what they do best.
We have learned to do nothing well.
We are still strangers to our bodies,

tools fit awkwardly in our hands, our weapons explode,
we speak to each other haltingly in words they gave us.

Taste what is in your mouth,
if it is water, still taste it.
Wash out the cups of your fingers,
clean your eyes with new tears for your sister.
We are not worse revolutionaries if we remember
that the universe itself pulses like a heart;
that the blood dances within us; that joy is a power
treading with hoofs and talons on our flimsy bodies;
that water flows and fire leaps and the land gives strength
if you build on it with respect, if you dance on it with vigor,
if you put seeds in with care and give back what is left over;
that a ritual of unity makes some of what it pretends;
that every thing is a part of something else.

The emperor

In the house of power grown old but unyielding
the emperor sits severe in mail, watching all that creep;
even over the grasshoppers and the minnows, over the leaves
that catch sun into food, he wields barrenness.
He holds a globe like something he might bite into
and an ankh, for he will carry his dominion into the living cells
and the ancient cabala of the genes he plans to revise
till everything born is programmed to obey.
The Man from Mars with sterile mountains at his back—
perhaps strip-mined, perhaps the site of weapons testing—
if we opened that armor like a can, would we find a robot?
quaking old flesh? the ghost of an inflated bond issue?

Evil old men banal as door knobs
who rule the world like a comic strip,
you are the Father Who Eats His Young.
Power abhors a vacuum, you say and sit down at the Wurlitzer
to play the color organ of poison gases.
All roads lead to the top of the pyramid on the dollar bill
where hearts are torn out and skulls split to feed
the ultimate ejaculating machine, the ruling class climax
          by missile.
The gnats of intelligence who have bugged every pay toilet
in the country sing in your beard of court cases and jails to come.
It is reason enough to bomb a village if it cannot be bought.
Heavy as dinosaurs, plated and armored,
you crush the land under your feet and flatten it.
Lakes of smoking asphalt spread where your feet have trod.

You exiled the Female into blacks and women and colonies.
You became the armed brain and the barbed penis and the club.
You invented agribusiness, leaching the soil to dust,
and pissed mercury in the rivers and shat slag on the plains,

withered your emotions to ulcers,
strait-jacketed the mysteries and sent them to shock therapy.
Your empress is a new-model car with breasts.

There is in the dance of all things together no profit
for each feeds the next and all pass through each other,
the serpent whose tail is in her mouth,
our mother earth turning.
Now the wheel of the seasons sticks and the circle is broken
and life spills out in an oil slick to rot the seas.
You are the God of the Puritans playing war games
        on computers:
you can give birth to nothing
except death.

The judgment

I call on the dead, I call on the defeated, on the starved,
the sold, the tortured, the executed, the robbed:
Indian women bayoneted before their children at Sand Creek,
miners who choked on the black lung,
strikers shot down at Pullman and Republic Steel,
women bled to death of abortions men made illegal,
sold, penned in asylums, lobotomized, raped and torn open,
every black killed by police, national guard, mobs and armies.
Live in us: give us your strength, give us your counsel,
give us your rage and your will to come at last into the light.

I fear the trial, I fear the struggle, it parches and withers me.
I fear the violence into whose teeth we march.
I long for the outcome with every cheated cell.
We shall all waken finally to being human.

I was trained to be numb, I was born to be numbered and pegged,
I was bred and conditioned to passivity, like a milk cow.
Waking is the sharpest pain I have ever known.
Every barrier that goes down takes part of my flesh
leaving me bloody. How can I live wide open?

Why must I think of you and you before I take a bite?
Why must I look to my sister before I scratch my itch?
I used to shuffle and giggle. I kept my eyes down
tucking my shoulders in so I would not rub the walls

of the rut, the place, the role.
Now anger blisters me.
My pride rumbles, sputtering lava.
Every day is dangerous and glad.

"Why do you choose to be noisy, to fight, to make trouble?"
you ask me, not understanding I have been born raw and new.
I can be killed with ease, I can be cut right down,
but I cannot crawl back in the cavern
where I lay with my neck bowed.
I have grown. I am not by myself.
I am too many.

The sun

Androgynous child whose hair curls into flowers,
naked you ride a horse without saddle or bridle
easy between your thighs from the walled garden outward.
Coarse sunflowers of desire whose seeds birds crack open
nod upon your journey, child of the morning whose sun
can only be born from us who strain bleeding to give birth.
Grow into your horse, let there be
no more riders or ridden.

Child, where are you heading with arms spread wide
as a shore, have I been there, have I seen that land shining
like sun spangles on clean water rippling?
I do not know your dances, I cannot translate your tongue
to words I use, your pleasures are strange to me
as the rites of bees: yet you are the yellow flower
of a melon vine growing out of my belly
though it climbs up where I cannot see in the strong light.

My eyes cannot decipher those shapes of children or
            burning clouds
who are not what we are: they go barefoot like savages,
they have computers as household pets; they are seven sexes
and only one sex; they do not own or lease or control.
They are of one body and of tribes. They are private as shamans
learning each her own magic at the teats of stones and trees.
They are all technicians and peasants.
They do not forget their birthright of self
or their mane of animal pride
dancing in and out through the gates of the body standing wide.

A bear lumbering, I waddle into the fields of their work games.
We are stunted slaves mumbling over the tales

of dragons our masters tell us, but we will be free.
Our children will be free of us uncomprehending
as we of those shufflers in caves who scraped for fire
and banded together at last to hunt the saber-toothed tiger,
the giant cave bear, predators
that had penned them up cowering so long.

The sun is rising, feel it: the air smells fresh.
I cannot look in the sun's face, its brightness blinds me,
but from my own shadow becoming distinct
I know that now at last
it is beginning to grow light.

BREAKING CAMP

HARD LOVING

4-TELLING

TO BE OF USE

From *LIVING IN THE OPEN*

Living in the open

1.

People ask questions
but never too many.
They are listening for the button to push
to make it go away.
They wait for me to confess
nights hollowed out with jealousy.

Or people say, Isn't that interesting
and believe nothing.
I must be public
as a dish of hors d'oeuvres on a bar.
I must hunt the shrubbery of couches for prey.
Loving not packaged in couples
shivers cracks down the closed world, the nuclear
egg of childhood, radioactive stone
at the base of the brain.

Can you imagine not having to lie?
To try to tell what you feel and want
till sometimes you can even see
each other clear and strange
as a photograph of your hand.

2.

We are all hustling and dealing
as we broil on the iron grates of the city.
Our minds charred, we collide and veer off.

Hard and spiny, we taste of DDT.
We trade each other in.
Talk is a poker game,

bed is a marketplace,
love is a soggy trap.

Property breeds theft and possession,
betrayal, the vinegar of contempt.
This woman, does she measure up?
This man, can I do better?
Each love is a purchase that can be returned
if it doesn't fit.

Hard as building a wall of sand.
Hard as gathering blackberries naked
in the thorny sprawl of a bramble.
Hard as saying I've made a mistake
and you were right.
How hard to love.
How painful to be friends.

My life frays into refuse,
parts of broken appliances,
into tapes recorded over, photographs
of people I no longer talk to
even on the phone.

How loud too the clash of my needs
in my pockets as I run to you
keys and coins jangling.
My hungers yowl and scrap in the gutter.
I will wring you for a few drops of reassurance.
My fears are telling the beads of your spine.
To hear your voice over the subway roar
of my will requires discipline.

No more lovers, no more husbands,
no masters or mistresses, contracts, no affairs,

only friends.
No more trade-ins or betrayals,
only the slow accretion of community,
hand on hand.

Help me to be clear and useful.
Help me to help you.
You are not my insurance, not my vacation,
not my romance, not my job, not my garden.
You wear your own flags and colors and your own names.
I will never have you.
I am a friend who loves you.

I awoke with the room cold

I awoke with the room cold and my cat
Arofa kneading my belly.
I had been walking around the lower east side
while from every alley and fruit market and stoop,
out from under the ravaged cars,
the cats came running to me.
All the cats had heard I was moving to the country
because of my lungs
and they began to cough and sneeze and whine.
All the starving rat-gnawed rickety spavined cats
of the lower east side with their fleas and worms
and their siren of hunger
followed me through the teeming blocks.
They threw themselves under the wheels of trucks
in an effort to keep up.
They were rubbing my ankles and yowling
that I must take every one of them along.
They wanted to breathe air that was not stained.
They wanted to roll on wet grass.
They wanted to chase a bird that wasn't a dirty pigeon.
Then the demands of the cats were drowned out.
As I ran, all of the eleven and twelve and thirteen year olds
who had died of skag in the smoking summer
began to miaou and miaou and miaou
till all of New York was white with pain like snow.

Gracious goodness

On the beach where we had been idly
telling the shell coins
cat's paw, cross-barred Venus, china cockle,
we both saw at once
the sea bird fall to the sand
and flap grotesquely.
He had taken a great barbed hook
out through the cheek and fixed
in the big wing.
He was pinned to himself to die,
a royal tern with a black crest blown back
as if he flew in his own private wind.
He felt good in my hands, not fragile
but muscular and glossy and strong,
the beak that could have split my hand
opening only to cry
as we yanked on the barbs.
We borrowed a clippers, cut and drew out the hook.
Then the royal tern took off, wavering,
lurched twice,
then acrobat returned to his element, dipped,
zoomed, and sailed out to dive for a fish.
Virtue: what a sunrise in the belly.
Why is there nothing
I have ever done with anybody
that seems to me so obviously right?

Homesick

Finally I have a house
where I return.
House half into the hillside,
wood that will weather to the wind's grey,
house built on sand
drawing water like a tree from its roots
where my roots too are set
and I return.

Where the men rode crosscountry on their dirt bikes in October
the hog cranberry will not grow back.
This land is vulnerable like my own flesh.
In New York the land seems cast out by a rolling mill
except where ancient gneiss pokes through.
Plains and mountain dwarf the human, seeming permanent,
but Indians were chasing mammoth with Folsom points
before glacial debris piled up Cape Cod where I return.

The colonists found beech and oak trees high as steeples
and chopped them down.
When Thoreau hiked from Sandwich outward
he crossed a desert
for they had farmed the land until it blew away
and slaughtered the whales and seals extinct.

Here you must make the frail dirt where your food grows.
Fertility is created of human castings and the sea's.
In the intertidal beach around each sand grain
swims a minute world dense with life.
Each oil slick wipes out galaxies.
Here we all lie on the palm of the poisoned sea our mother
where life began and is now ending
and we return.

146

Seedlings in the mail

Like mail order brides
they are lacking in glamor.
Drooping and frail and wispy,
they are orphaned waifs of some green catastrophe
from which only they have been blown to safety
swaddled in a few wraiths of sphagnum moss.
Windbreaks, orchards, forests of the mind
they huddle in the dirt
smaller than our cats.
The catalog said they would grow
to stand one hundred feet tall.
I could plant them in the bathroom.
I could grow them in window pots,
twelve trees to an egg carton.
I could dig four into the pockets of my jeans.
I could wear some in my hair
or my armpits.
Ah, for people like us, followed
by forwarding addresses and dossiers and limping causes
it takes a crazy despairing faith
full of teeth as a jack o'lantern
to plant pine and fir and beech
for somebody else's grandchildren,
if there are any.

The daily life of the worker bee

We breed plants, order seeds from
the opulent pornography of the catalogs,
plant, weed, fertilize, water.
But the flowers do not shine for us.

Forty days of life, working like a housewife
with six kids in diapers, at it like an oil rig pumping.
With condescension we pass on : busy as a bee.

Yet for them the green will of the plants
has thrust out colors, odors, the shapely trumpets and cups.
As the sun strikes the petals, the flower uncurls,
the bees come glinting and singing.

Now she crawls into the crimson rooms of the rose
where perfume reddens the air to port wine.
Marigolds sturdy in the grass barking like golden chow dogs
cry their wares to her. Enter. Devour me!
In her faceted eyes each image reverberates.
Cumulus clouds of white phlox
pile up for her in the heat of the sunburnt day.
Down into the soft well of the summer lilies,
cerise, citron, umber, rufous orange,
anthers with their palate of pollen
tremble as she enters.
She rubs her quivering fur

into each blue bell of the borage.
In the chamber of the peony she is massaged with silk.

Forty days she is drunk with nectar.
Each blossom utters fragrance to entice her,
offers up its soft flanks, its maddening colors,
its sweet and pungent fluids.
She never mates : her life is orgasm of all senses.
She dies one morning exhausted in the lap of the rose.
Like love letters turned up in an attic trunk
her honey remains to sweeten us.

Cod summer

June is the floodtide of green,
wet and lush and leafy, heavyladen.
In full summer the grass bleaches
to sand, hue of grasshoppers on the dunes.
The marsh begins to bronze.

Hot salty afternoons : the sun
stuns. Drops on our heads like a stone.
Among the pitch pines the sparse shade
simmers with resin.
Crickets shiver the air.
The path is white sand shimmering
leading down from the hill of scrub oak
crusty with lichens, reindeer moss,
ripe earth stars scattering their spores.

Nothing commands the eye
except the sea at the horizon.
We must actively look : textures
of ground cover, poverty grass, bearberry,
lowbush blueberry, wood lily, Virginia rose.
The dusty beach plums range on the gnarled branch
from soft dull green through blush and purple
like a tourist's sunset in miniature.

Sandy, dwarfed, particular
this landscape yields nothing from a car.
A salt marsh must be learned on foot, wading,

lumbering in the muck, hopping tussocks of salt meadow grass,
hay arising sideways from last year's fallen harvest.
The marsh clicks and rustles
with fiddler crabs scuttling to their holes.
The blue-eyed grass has bloomed.
Now we find fat joints of samphire
turning orange, the intricate sea lavender.
Under us the tide undulates
percolating through the layers, slithering
with its smell of life feeding and renewing
like my own flesh after sex.

We go in this landscape together learning it
barefoot and studious with our guides in a knapsack
catching Fowler's toads and letting them go.

A proposal for recycling wastes

Victim not of an accident
but of a life that was accidental
she sprawls on the nursing
home bed : has a photo
of herself at seventeen with long
brown hair, face paprikaed
with freckles, like a granddaughter
who may live
in San Diego. In Decatur
love picked her up
by the scruff and after
out of work wandering dumped
her in Back of the Yards Chicago.
A broken nose, the scar of love;
stretch marks and a tooth lost
each child, love like
tuberculosis, it happens.
And generation used
her like a rutted highway
the heavy trucks trundling
their burdens all day and all
night. Her body was a thing
stuffed, swollen, convulsed
empty, producing for the state
and Jesus three soldiers and one
sailor, two more breeding wombs
and a (defunct) prostitute.
The surviving corporal drives
hack, one mother waits tables;

the other typed, married into
the suburbs and is den
mother to cubscouts.
The husband, cocksman, luckless
horse and numbersplayer, security
guard and petty thief, died
at fifty-six of cancer
of the colon.
Now like an abandoned car
she has been towed here
to fall apart.
She wastes, drugged,
in a spreading pool
of urine.
Surely she could be used,
her eyes, her heart
still strangely sturdy,
her one good kidney
could be salvaged for the rich
who are too valuable at seventy-four
to throw away.

The bumpity road
to mutual devotion

Do you remember the first raw winter
of our women's group, both of us fierce as mother bears?
Every day came down like a pile driver in the morning
shaking the bed empty
stomping sleep like a run-over bag.
Our pain was new, a too sharp kitchen knife.
We bled on everything we touched.
I could hardly type for scars.
Rage sang like a coloratura doing trills
in my head as I ricocheted up male streets.
You came on like a sergeant of marines.
You were freshly ashamed of your beauty
believing if you frowned a lot no one
would notice your face.
The group defined us the strong ones
loved us, hated us, baited us, set us
one on the other. We met
almost clandestinely. You brought flowers.
We praised lesbian love intellectually, looking
hard in each other's black eyes, and each stayed
on her side of the kitchen exuding
a nervous whine like an avalanche of white mice.

What a rutted road through thick gassy clouds of nightmare,
political bedlam. Each has let
the other down and picked her up.
We will never be lovers; too scared
of losing each other. What tantalizes past flesh
—too mirrored, lush, dark haired and soft in the belly—
is the strange mind rasping, clanging, engaging.
What we fantasize—rising like a bird kite
on the hot afternoon air—is work together.
Projects, battles, schemes, manifestoes

are born from the brushing of wills
like small sparks from loose hair,
and will we let them fade, static electricity?

What shall we do before
they crush us? How far will we travel
to no country on earth?
What houses should we build? and which tear down?
what chapels, what bridges, what power stations
and stations of that burning green energy
beyond the destruction of power?
Trust me with your hand. For us to be friends
is a mating of eagle and ostrich, from both sides.

On Castle Hill

As we wandered through the hill of graves,
men lost at sea, women in childbirth,
slabs on which were thriftily listed
nine children like drowned puppies,
all the Susan-B-wife-of-Joshua-Stones,
a woman in a long calico gown strolled toward us
bells jangling at waist, at wrists,
lank brown hair streaming.
We spoke to her but she smiled only
and drifted on into the overgrown woods.
Suppose, you said, she is a ghost.
You repeated a tale from Castanada
about journeying toward one's childhood
never arriving but encountering
on the way many people, all dead,
journeying toward the land of heart's desire.

I would not walk a foot into my childhood,
I said, picking blackberries for you to taste,
large, moist and sweet as your eyes.
My land of desire is the marches
of the unborn. The dead
are powerless to grant us
wishes, their struggles
are the wave that carried us here.
Our wind blows on toward those hills
we will never see.

From *Sand Roads*

7. The development

The bulldozers come, they rip
a hole in the sand along
the new blacktop road with a tony name
(Trotting Park, Pamet Hills)
and up goes another glass-walled-
split-level-livingroom-vast-as-a-
roller-rink-$100,000
summer home for a psychiatrist
and family.

Nine months vacation homes
stand empty except for mice
and spiders, an occasional
bird with a broken back twitching
on the deck under a gape of glass.

I live in such a development
way at the end of a winding
road where the marsh begins
to close in: two houses,
the one next door a local
fisherman lost to the bank
last winter, ours a box
half buried in the sand.
This land is rendered
too expensive
to live on. We feed
four people off it,
a kind of organic tall corn
ornery joke at road's end.
We planted for the birds cover
and berries, we compost, we set out
trees and at night

the raccoons come shambling.
Yet the foxes left us,
shrinking into the marsh.
I found their new den.
I don't show it
to anyone.
Forgive us, grey fox, our stealing
your home, our loving
this land carved into lots
over a shrinking watertable
where the long sea wind that blows
the sand whispers to developers
money, money, money.

8. The road behind the last dune

Mostly you don't see the ocean
although when the surf is up
its roaring fills you
like a shell,
whistling through your
ears, your bones.

Nothing stands up here
but you, in the steady
rasp of the salt wind.
The oaks grow a foot high
dry gnarled jungles
you can't wade through
where eyes watch.
The hog cranberry bronze
in the fall, shines

metallically revealing
every hump.
The dune grass ripples
like a pelt, and around every
clump is traced a circle,
fingers of the wind.
Fox grape on the high dunes,
poison ivy whose bright berries
the birds carry in their bodies
to scatter, the dune
colored grasshoppers,
the fox with fur of fine sand.

You are standing too tall for
this landscape. Lie down.
Let the grass blow
over you. Let the plover
pipe, the kestrel stand beating its wings
in the air, the wolf spider
come to the door of its burrow,
the mouse nibble on
your toe. Let the beach pea
entangle your legs in its vine
and ring you with purple blossoms.

Now get up slowly
and seek a way down off the dunes,
carefully : your heavy feet
assault the balance.
Come down on the bench
of the great beach arching

away into fog.
Lie down before the ocean.
It rises over you, it stands
hissing and spreading its
cobalt hood, rattling
its pebbles.
Cold it is and its rhythm
as it eats away the beach,
as it washes the dunes out to sea
to build new spits and islands,
enters your blood and slows
the beat of that newish contraption
your heart controlling the waves
of your inward salt sea.
Let your mind open
like a clam when the waters
slide back to feed it.
Flow out to the ancient cold
mothering embrace, cold
and weightless yourself
as a fish, over the buried
wrecks. Then with respect
let the breakers drive you
up and out into
the heavy air, your heart
pounding. The warm scratchy sand
like a receiving blanket
holds you up gasping with life.

Rough times

for Nancy Henley

We are trying to live
as if we were an experiment
conducted by the future,

blasting cell walls
that no protective seal or inhibition
has evolved to replace.

I am conducting a slow vivisection
on my own tissues, carried out
under the barking muzzle of guns.

Those who speak of good and simple
in the same sandwich of tongue and teeth
inhabit some other universe.

Good draws blood from my scalp and files my nerves.
Good runs the yard engine of the night over my bed.
Good pickles me in the brown vinegar of guilt.
Good robs the easy words as they rattle off my teeth,
leaving me naked as an egg.

Remember that pregnancy is beautiful only
at a distance from the distended belly.
A new idea rarely is born like Venus attended by graces.
More commonly it's modeled of baling wire and acne.
More commonly it wheezes and tips over.

Most mutants die: only
a minority refract the race
through the prisms of their genes.

Those slimy fish with air sacs were ugly
as they hauled up on the mud flats
heaving and gasping. How clumsy we are
in this new air we reach with such effort
and cannot yet breathe.

161

Phyllis wounded

To fight history as it carries us,
to swim upstream across the currents—no!—
to move the river, to create new currents
with the force of our arms and backs,
to shape this torrent as it shapes us
flowing, churning, dragging us under
into the green moil where the breath is pummeled
from the lungs and the eyes burst backward,
among rocks, the teeth of the white water
grinning like hungry bears,
ah, Phyllis, you complain too much!

We all carry in the gold lockets
of the good birthday child sentimental
landscapes in pale mauve where we have
everything we desire carried in on trays
serene as jade buddhas,
respectable as Jane Austen,
secure as an obituary in the *Times*.

We were not made for a heaven of Sundays.
Most people are given hunger, the dim pain
of being used twisting through the bowels,
close walls and a low sky, troubles visited
from above like tornadoes that level the house,
pain early, pain late, and a death not chosen.

My friend, the amazons were hideous
with the white scars of knife wounds,
the welts of sword slashes, flesh that would
remind nobody of a ripe peach.
But age sucks us all dry.

Old campaigners waken to the resonant singing
of angels of pillars of fire and pillars of ash

that only trouble the sleep of women
who climb on a platform or crouch at a barricade.
Your smile is rich with risk
and subtle with enemies contested.
Your memories whistle and clang and moan
in the dark like buoys that summon
and give warning of danger
and the channel through.

I was not born a serf bound to a ryefield,
I was not born to bend over a pressing machine
in a loft while the sun rose and set, I was not born
to starve in the first year with big
belly and spindly legs, I was not born
to be gang raped by soldiers at fourteen,
I was not born to die in childbirth,
to be burned at the stake by the Church,
but of all these we are the daughters
born of luck round as an apple
and fat as a goose, to charge into battle
swinging our great-grandmother's bones.
Millions of dead women keen in our hair
for food and freedom, the electricity
drives me humming. What privilege
to be the heiresses of so much wanting!
How can we ever give up?

Our laughter has been honed by adversity
till it gleams like an ax
and we will not die by our own hand.

Rape poem

There is no difference between being raped
and being pushed down a flight of cement steps
except that the wounds also bleed inside.

There is no difference between being raped
and being run over by a truck
except that afterward men ask if you enjoyed it.

There is no difference between being raped
and being bit on the ankle by a rattlesnake
except that people ask if your skirt was short
and why you were out alone anyhow.

There is no difference between being raped
and going head first through a windshield
except that afterward you are afraid
not of cars
but half the human race.

The rapist is your boyfriend's brother.
He sits beside you in the movies eating popcorn.
Rape fattens on the fantasies of the normal male
like a maggot in garbage.

Fear of rape is a cold wind blowing
all of the time on a woman's hunched back.
Never to stroll alone on a sand road through pine woods,
never to climb a trail across a bald
without that aluminum in the mouth
when I see a man climbing toward me.

Never to open the door to a knock
without that razor just grazing the throat.
The fear of the dark side of hedges,

the back seat of the car, the empty house
rattling keys like a snake's warning.
The fear of the smiling man
in whose pocket is a knife.
The fear of the serious man
in whose fist is locked hatred.

All it takes to cast a rapist is seeing your body
as jackhammer, as blowtorch, as adding-machine-gun.
All it takes is hating that body
your own, your self, your muscle that softens to flab.

All it takes is to push what you hate,
what you fear onto the soft alien flesh.
To bucket out invincible as a tank
armored with treads without senses
to possess and punish in one act,
to rip up pleasure, to murder those who dare
live in the leafy flesh open to love.

The consumer

My eyes catch and stick
as I wade in bellysoft heat.
Tree of miniature chocolates filled with liqueur,
tree of earrings tinkling in the mink wind,
of Bach oratorios spinning light at 33⅓,
tree of Thailand silks murmuring changes.
Pluck, eat and grow heavy.
From each hair a wine bottle dangles.
A toaster is strung through my nose.
An elevator is installed in my spine.
The mouth of the empire
eats onward through the apple of all.
Armies of brown men
are roasted into coffee beans,
are melted into chocolate,
are pounded into copper.
Their blood is refined into oil,
black river oozing rainbows
of affluence.
Their bodies shrink
to grains of rice.
I have lost my knees.
I am the soft mouth of the caterpillar.
People and landscapes are my food
and I grow fat and blind.

The provocation of the dream

In the suburbs of the ganglia,
in the tract houses of the split-level brain,
in the bulldozed bowling alleys where staked saplings
shiver like ostriches in a zoo,
on streets empty of people
that dead-end at the expressway where cars bullet by,
in egg carton bedrooms, the dream is secreted.

On the clambering vines of the fingers
hard green dreams shape around seeds.
Sour enough to scald the tongue,
bitter with tannin and acid,
hard as granite chips, will these grapes ripen to give wine?

In the red Tau of the womb
dreams clot, clump, a dense pale smear
like a nebula.
Who has known this woman?
This woman has known herself.

The wind impregnated me,
the wind galloping with tangled mane through the brush
with burrs snarled in the shimmering coat.
The wind fills me, I am her sail and shoot before.
The wind slips through the tawny feathered grass
and enters my breath.

Six hours after I had dropped acid
I began to labor. I was brought to a room with men
and a woman who belonged to the men.
Mosquito fears bothered them.
They held me down till my muscles tore
but I was granted blindness.
The drum of my uterus pounded.
The fist of my womb clenched and unclenched

on me, in the surging cave.
Death crooned under the roar of the waterfall
calling to the child to rest, to stay, to sleep;
calling to the mother to falter, to sink, to fade.

Weeping and screaming I gave birth, I was born.
When I came down
I was handed shame like a cup of sour coffee
for the noise I had made when I had not known them,
when I had been knowing myself.
In the proper ritual we change roles and give assistance.
We bring each other through on that wind.

In the dim tunnels of library stacks
the dream is laid in the spines of books
like the eggs of beetles, in fairy stories,
broken statues and painted vases, mythologies,
legends of queens, old wives' tales.
The eggs hatch larvae who chew and change.

The dream advances like a wave of purple dye
through the conduits of the blood.
The vision alters dreams till the night is hung
with bold faces painted on shields,
the voices of women like bright scarves on the wind,
the cries of women wet as blood,
women who dance in fire burning and charred
but still dance
together.

I wait for the dream to enter the brain
and turn on the power to connect,
clearing the roads of the instincts.
The fountains will run water and the fruit of the senses

offer its sweetness and knowledge on every stall.
The office workers will go out to the green belt to plant
and the peasants of the belly will also give law.

I wait for the dream to reach the eyes
and shatter the mirror where the moon of the face
eclipses energy's sun.
I wait for the dream to reach the belly
and make us serious as lean grey wolves
whose shadows race far behind as they hunt.
I wait for the dream to enter the muscles
till we ride our anger like elephants into battle.

We are sleep walkers troubled by nightmare flashes.
In locked wards, we closet our vision, renouncing.
We turn love loud on the radio to shut out cries in the street.
Ours is the sleep of objects given, sold, taken, discarded,
a shuddering sleep whose half remembered dreams
are cast on the neat lawn of the domestic morning,
red blossoms torn by a high wind from a crab apple tree.
Only when we break the mirror and climb into our vision,
only when we are the wind together streaming and singing,
only in the dream we become with our bones for spears,
we are real at last
and wake.

Looking at quilts

Who decided what is useful in its beauty
means less than what has no function besides beauty
(except its weight in money)?
Art without frames: it held parched corn,
it covered the table where soup misted savor,
it covered the bed where the body knit
to self and other and the
dark wool of dreams.

The love of the ordinary blazes out: the backyard
miracle: Ohio Sunflower,
                          Snail's Track,
                                          Sweet Gum Leaf,
                          Moon over the Mountain.

In the pattern Tulip and Peony the sense
of design masters the essence of what sprawled
in the afternoon: called conventionalized
to render out the choice, the graphic wit.

Some have a wistful faded posy yearning:
                                          Star of the Four Winds,
                          Star of the West,
                                          Queen Charlotte's Crown.
In a crabbed humor as far from pompous
as a rolling pin, you can trace wrinkles
from smiling under a scorching grasshopper sun:
                          Monkey Wrench,
                                          The Drunkard's Path,
                                                          Fool's Puzzle,

Puss in the Corner,
                    Robbing Peter to Pay Paul,
and the deflating
                    Hearts and Gizzards.

Pieced quilts, patchwork from best gowns,
winter woolens, linens, blankets, worked jigsaw
of the memories of braided lives, precious
scraps : women were buried but their clothing wore on.

Out of death from childbirth at sixteen, hard
work at forty, out of love for the trumpet vine
and the melon, they issue to us :
                    Rocky Road to Kansas,
          Job's Troubles,
                    Crazy Ann,
                         The Double Irish Chain,
          The Tree of Life :
                    this quilt might be
the only perfect artifact a woman
would ever see, yet she did not doubt
what we had forgotten, that out of her
potatoes and colic, sawdust and blood
she could create ; together, alone,
she seized her time and made new.

To the pay toilet

You strop my anger, especially
when I find you in restaurant or bar
and pay for the same liquid, coming and going.
In bus depots and airports and turnpike plazas
some woman is dragging in with three kids hung off her
shrieking their simple urgency like gulls.
She's supposed to pay for each of them
and the privilege of not dirtying the corporate floor.
Sometimes a woman in a uniform's on duty
black or whatever the prevailing bottom is
getting thirty cents an hour to make sure
no woman sneaks her full bladder under a door.
Most blatantly you shout that waste of resources
for the greatest good of the smallest number
where twenty pay toilets line up glinty clean
and at the end of the row one free toilet
oozes from under its crooked door,
while a row of weary women carrying packages and babies
wait and wait and wait to do
what only the dead find unnecessary.

All clear

Loss is also clearance.
Emptiness is also receptivity.
No, I cannot pretend:
the cells of my body lack you
and keen their specific hunger.
Yet, a light slants over this bleak landscape
from the low yellow sun,
a burning kite caught in the branches.
There is a lightness in me, the absence
of the weight of your judgment
bearing on my nape,
the slow stain of your judgment
rusting the moment.
I go out with empty hands
and women touch me, lightly, while we talk.
The words, the problems, the sharp faces
jostle like winter birds at a feeding station
although the crumpled fields look deserted.
I stroll in the cold gelid morning.

When it becomes clear I am not replacing you
don't think it is primarily
because you cannot be replaced.
Consider that I am taking pleasure
in space, visited but unoccupied
for every man I have loved
was like an army.

∡ench yourself

              ₊ove, open.
ı ₍   you we are able
I tell you we are able
now and then gently
with hands and feet
cold even as fish
to curl into a tangle
and grow a single hide,
slowly to unknit all other skin
and rest in flesh
and rest in flesh entire.
Come all the way in, love,
it is a river
with a strong current
but its brown waters
will not drown you.
Let go.
Do not hold out
your head.
The current knows the bottom
better than your feet can.
You will find
that in this river
we can breathe
we can breathe
and under water see
small gardens and bright fish
too tender
too tender
for the air.

The homely war

1.

Wrote two letters while rain
trickled in lean streaks down my window.
One crowed of friends hiking, steamers, hot pie,
fat with bobwhite, peas planted and rhubarb dug in.
There are facts offered in the hand like ripe raspberries,
common phrases gentle as the caress of trailing hair.

The other malingered in a recitativo of wrongs,
counterpoint of minor and major abuse
quavering on a few tones of No.
A defense after my execution, a sense
that catches on the lip like a chipped glass
of having been used : used like a coin in a slot
or a borrowed towel slung sopping on a chair.
Tanglement that broke raw, in physical threat.
Months later the lies still come back
letters battered and stained, from a false address.

Happiness is simple
a box of sunshine
body against body, closed circuit of response.
Only misery is so complicated.

When another year turns over
compost in the pile
last year's feast breeding knots of juicy worms,
I do not want to be indicting
new accusations to another exlover
who has thrown off the scarlet cloak of desire to reveal
the same skeletal coldness, the need to control
crouching like an adding machine in his eyes,
the same damp doggy hatred of women,
the eggshell ego and the sandpaper touch,

the boyish murderer spitting mommy on his bayonet.
I am tired of finding my enemy in my bed.

2.

For two years I broke from these cycles, simply.
I thought the death of sex would quiet the air to crystal.
I would see what there was between women and men
besides itch, dependency, habit.

I learned less than I expected.
Judgment sat on my shoulder like a pet crow.
My dreams were skim milk and albumin.
I lacked irrational joy, a lion
lying on my chest purring, the hawk's talons and cry,
the coarse glory of the daylily that every midsummer morning
raises a new trumpet, that withers with dusk.
My head was severed like a flower in a glass
that would never make seeds.
Like an oak my tap goes deep,
more of me is in the earth than spread into air.
I think best rooted grappling past words.

Better, I thought, for me in my rough being
to force makeshift connections,
patches, encounters, rows,
better to swim in trouble like a muddy river rising
than to become at last all thesis
correct, consistent but hollow
the finished ghost
of my own struggle.

3.

Madeline, in your purity I find myself rebuked.
Madeline, in your clarity I find myself restored.
You are the stream that breaks out
of a living tree; like the peach
you open your blossoms
to the wind that bears frost
a knife in its teeth,
you bloom in a ravaged landscape
black spring
old deaths coming to light
bones and split bellies of hunger,
the remaindered pages of the fall.
You stand and open from bare wood
fertile alone like the peach tree.
Long delicate leaves, slim green moons,
ripple over the sweet fruit
rounding on its stones.

You strike on marble at the core, rock
metamorphosed in pain and pressure,
the texture of agonized flesh.
You are vulnerable as the first buds of the maple
the deer arch their necks to crop.

Delicacy and honesty, unicorn and amazon wrestle
in your high sugar maple forest,
the Vermont hillside you love,
hard wood that drips sweetness you mistrust,
the symmetrical sculpture of each leaf,
the dome of the summer tree
heavy and dense as syrup, as sleep.

You grow deep into your rock, down into the cold
crevices of the fear of first and last things.
The stone of your death you crack and enter

with your lightning brain, with your fingers that ache.
Pain is the familiar whispering in your ear.

I come with my raggedy loves dragging
into the sphere of your clear regard.
I praise our common fight.
I praise friendship embarked on suddenly as a bus that arrives.
I praise friendship maturing like a tall beech tree.
I praise the differences that define us.
I love what I cannot be
as well as what I am.

4.

Seeking from women nurturance, feedback, idea,
my politics, my collective, why then this
open frontier with men? Yet I tell you in the other
I meet the dream exotic as a dragonfly's eye,
the grenade of a phrase, the joke that would never
leap the gap of the poles of my mind,
the angers struck unexpected
a spade clanging on rock in sand.
Talking without words on the body's drum:
it is flat, it is woody, it is lean as a shark's belly,
spiny as a sea urchin, leathery, gross, tulip sleek,
fur of the hare or wool of the sheep,
the toadstool of sex raising its ruddy bald head.
I find you beautiful, I find you funny, I find
you not translatable to words of my blood.
In that meeting I seep
out to the limits where my ego fades
into flesh, into electricity of the muscles thrumming,
into light patterns imploding on the nerves,
into the wet caves where my strength is born again.

I never want to merge: only to overlap,
to grow sensitive in the moment so that we move

together as currents, so that carried
on that wave we sense skin upon skin
nerve into nerve with millions of tiny windows
open to each other's light as we shine
from the nebulous center like squid
and then let go.

5.

I lack a light touch.
I step on my own words,
a garden rake in the weeds.
I sweat and heave when I should slip away.
I am earnest into sermons when I should shrug.
I ram on.

The inhabitants of my life change,
tides in a subway car.
At every stop coming and going.
What is constant except a few travelers
in the same direction, and the will to continue
through the loud dark
in the hope of someday arriving?

6.

My old friend, how we sustain
each other, how we bear witness.
We are each other's light luggage of essentials.
We are each other's film archive and museum
packed in the crumbling arch of the skull.
Trust is the slowest strength, growing
microscopic ring on ring of living wood.
The greater gift is caring,
the laying on of hands in the dark,
of words in the light.
The lesser gift is remembering,

the compass in the bush that makes clear the way
come, the way to go.
We have shaped each other.

My new friend, every beginning throws the scent
of a sunny morning in a pine grove after rain.
The senses stretch out the necks of giraffes
for the smallest leaf of data to understand.
We give with the doors wide open;
a gardener with too many tomatoes,
we count nothing, we fill bushels with joy.
When does the tallying start?
Slowly underground fears begin, invisible
as the mycelium of a toadstool
waiting only for a damp morning to sprout.
I ask you to give much, to give up more.
What comes easy to a man comes
out of women. Nothing will be easy here.
Good will starts out fat and sweet
as tub butter and turns slowly rancid.
It must be made again daily
if we want it fresh.

The waters of trust run as deep as the river of fear
through the dark caverns in the bone.
Work is my center, my trunk
yet we are rooted in loving connection
with a deep grasping and full green giving.

7.

I am sick, sick to desperation
of the old defeats, of the broken treaties,
episodes of the same colonial war of women and men.
I want the cavalry to take off those bemedaled blue uniforms

180

the color of Zeus and those shiny boots clanking with spurs.
I want the horses to win this time and eat grass together.

In this movie the Army always comes bugling over the hill,
burns some squaws and pens up the rest on a reservation,
paves over the sacred dancing ground for a Stop and Shop,
and a ten-lane turnpike to the snowmobile factory.
Then they ask the doctor why nothing is fun.
Their eyes are the color of television screens.
They come by pretending, they die with their minds turned off.

Do you think on the tenting ground of General Bluster
young renegades may begin to steal away?
Or will they always go back for their paychecks?
I think it is time for the extras to burn down the movie.

Yes, I am sick of treaties with the enemy who brings to bed
his boots and his law, who is
still and after my enemy.
I have been trained to love him, and he to use me.
Yes, I am weary of war where I want exchange,
sick of harvesting disgust from the shoots of joy.
Fight with my tribe or die in your blue uniform
but don't think you can take it off in bed.
It dyes your words, your brain runs cobalt
and your tear ducts atrophy to pebbles.

I love easily: never mind that.
Love is the paper script of this loose army.
Let us sleep on honesty at night like a board.
Talk with your body, talk with your life.
Grow me good will
rough and thick as meadow grass
but tend it like an invalid house plant,
a tender African violet in the best window.

181

The twelve-spoked wheel flashing

A turn of the wheel, I thrust
up with effort pushing, braced and sweating,
then easy over down into sleep, body idle,
and the sweet loamy smell of the earth,
a turn of the twelve-spoked wheel flashing.

I have tried to forge my life whole,
round, integral as the earth spinning.
I have tried to bet my values,
poker played with a tarot deck,
all we hope and fear and struggle for,
where the white chips are the eyes of anguish,
the red the coins of blood paid on the streets
and the blues are all piled by the dealer.
We sit round the table gambling against the house:
the power hidden under the green felt,
the television camera that reads your hand,
the magnetic dice, the transistorized
computer controlled deck that riffles
with the sound of ice
blowing on the wind against glass.

A turn of the wheel: nothing
stays. The redwinged blackbirds implode
into a tree above the salt marsh one
March day piping and chittering
every year, but the banded pet
does not return. The cherry tree begins
to bear this June, a cluster
of sweet black fruit warm on the palm.
The rue died of the winter heaves.
We'll plant a new one. It does not
taste the same, bitter always, but
even in bitterness there are shades,

flavors, subtle essences, discretions
in what sets the teeth on edge.

Down into the mud of pain,
buried, choking, shivering with despair,
the fire gone out in the belly's hearth
and frogs hopping on the floor,
ears sealed with icy muck,
and the busy shrill cricket of the mad
ego twitching its legs in dry
compulsion all night. Up into the sun
that ripens you like a pear
bronze and golden, the hope that twines
its strands clambering up to the light
and bears fragrant wide blossoms opening
like singing faces.

Turn and turn again and turn,
always rolling on with massive thumps
and sudden lurching dives, I am pinned
to the wheel of the seasons,
hot and cold, sober and glad and menacing,
bearing and losing. I turn head high,
head low, my feet brushing the pine boughs,
moss in my ears, my nose gathering
snow, my feet soaked like a tree's
roots. I go rolling on, heads and tails,
turn and turn again and turn,
pinned to the wheel of my choice and choosing still,
stretched on the wheel of the seasons,
learning and forgetting and moving
some part of the way toward
a new and better place, some part
of the way toward dying.

What the owl sees

Mirror from the twenties
in a gilded frame muting
pleasantly dull, you hung
over the secondhand buffet
in the diningroom
that proved we were practically
middleclass : table with claw
legs, cave of genteel lace.
Underneath I crawled
running my toy car.

In that asbestos box
no room was big enough
to pace more than one stride.
When we shut up we could hear
neighbors in multifamily cages
six feet each side, yelling.
We could smell the liver
and onions frying, we could
hear the tubercular cough
racking an old man's lungs.

When the sun hit your
beveled edge, rainbows would
quiver out to stripe the walls
clear as sugar candy, pure as
the cry of my hunger.

Now you hang in this rented
space, my only heirloom, over
a radiator, and as I rise

I see my naked body
poised in you like a diver
about to leap.

Your carved frame in childhood
I feared as an owl's head,
eyes of a predator.
You carry in your depths
like mouse bones the starving
blue face of that
unwanted brat. Survival
knocks and hisses.
                        I still
see the wooden owl staring
but beneath I recognize
your sides are gently
curved in and out
female as my own facing
me inside you. I smile
at you, at me, at
that battered surviving heiress
of mousebone soup.

The Greater Grand Rapids lover

In all of Greater Grand Rapids you
are the only one who knows me
the shape of my thighs and my fears
working like yeast
the taste of my laughter
how my teeth chatter
in a cold wind of despairing.

Slowly I evaporate here
drying into a paper scarecrow,
simplified into a scaffolding
of pipes in which a neon
womanfist blinks. I am all
facade and fixed grimaces
like a pinochle deck.

My blood is slowing with
the wide cold brown river.
My frog heart burrows
deep in the mud of the bank.
My hands fold up
and harden on sticks to wait for spring.
My voice flies out over
the stiff grasses of the field
searching and comes back hungry.

Here you have fourteen lovers
and I only one. At home
I have fourteen lovers but here only you
precious as drops of winter sun.
Have you had your vitamin C,
I ask you, take another piece of
chicken, let me massage you,

solicitous as an heir
fingering a parchment will.

Curious as snails meeting on a gate
we exchange with soft horns
and wet organs, words and signals,
information, tricks, the history of the soft
flowing foot and the intricate
masonry bower of shell. How the strange
minds twine and glitter and swing
looped in words like a hammock.
How the strange minds joining stand,
charmed snakes glittering
to dance their knowledge.

Round and round I turn
in you, a cat making a bed,
kneading you with my velvet and claws,
butting and nudging and licking,
round and round, and my hair
grows another foot and my eyes
shine gold and red like a carnival.
Then I walk outside and the cold
wind plucks the fur and the shine
from all the branches of my bones.

The Lansing bad penny come again blues

So you turn up like an old
arrest record, so you turn
up like a single boot
after I finally threw the other
away, so you turn up
like a drunken wobbly angel
making your own fierce annunciation
to this wilting female
trouble, garlands of trouble.

Tomorrow you go to jail
and tonight you sit before me
brushing me with the gaze
of your eyes burning
and smoky: your eyes that
change, grey into blue,
and that look that never changes.

*Lately I haven't thought
of you every day, lately it hasn't
been as bad,* you say, and
when I laugh, your mouth
calls me cruel.

Ah, you chew your heart
like a steak rare and salty.
When you are cozy in my bed
you twitch with restlessness,
you want to be mirroring your
face in shopwindows in Port
au Prince. When you are gone
a thousand miles you wake up

with the veins of your arm
boring like sirens, and you
want me night and morning
till your belly wrings dry.

I am simple and dogged
as a turtle crossing a road
while you dance jagged epicycles
around me. Now you are
laughing because you know
how to unzip shells. For a few
hours we will both get
just what we want: this is Act
Forty Four in a play
that would be tedious to observers
but for us strict
and necessary as a bullfight,
a duel, the dance of double
suns, twinned stars
whose attraction and repulsion
balance as they inscribe
erratic orbits whose center
is where the other was
or will be.

The poet dreams of a nice warm motel

Of course the plane is late
two hours twisting bumpily
over Chicago in a droning grey funk
with the seatbelt sign on.
Either you are met by seven
young Marxists who want to know
at once What Is To Be Done
or one professor who says, What?
You have luggage? But I
parked in the no
parking zone.

Oh, we wouldn't want to put you
up at a motel, we here at
Southwestern Orthodontic Methodist,
we want you to feel homey:
drafty rooms where icicles
drip on your forehead, dorm cubicles
under the belltower where
the bells boom all night on each
quarter hour, rooms in faculty attics
two miles from a bathroom.
                              The bed
is a quarter inch mattress
flung upon springs of upended
razor blades: the mattress
is stuffed with fingernail
clippings and the feathers of buzzards.
If you roll over or cough it
sounds like a five car collision.

The mattress is shaped that way
because our pet hippo Sweetie
likes to nap there. It's homey,

isn't it, meaning we're going to keep
you up with instant coffee
until two A.M. discussing why
we at Middle Fork State Teachers College
don't think you are truly great.

You'll love our dog Ogre,
she adores sleeping with guests
especially when she's in heat.
Don't worry, the children
will wake you. (They do.)
In the morning while all
fourteen children (the ones
with the flu and whooping cough
and oh, you haven't had
the mumps—I mean, yet?) assault
you with tomahawks and strawberry
jam, you are asked, oh
would you like breakfast?
Naturally we never eat
breakfast ourselves, we believe
fasting purifies the system.
Have some cold tofu,
don't mind the mold.

No, we didn't order
your books, that's rampant
commercialism. We will call you
Miz Percy and make a joke about
women's libbers. The mike was run
over by a snowplow.
If we were too busy to put
up posters, we've obtained the
outdoor Greek Amphitheater

194

where you'll read to me and my wife.
If we blanketed five states
with announcements, we will be astounded
when five hundred cram into
the women's restroom we reserved.

Oh yes, the check will be four
months late. The next hungry poet
will be told, you'll be real comfortable
here, What's-her-name, she wrote that book
The Flying Dyke, she was through last year
and she found it real homey
in the Athens of the West.

Skimpy day at the solstice

The whiskey-colored sun
cruises low as a marshhawk
over the dun grass.
Long intricate shadows bar the path.

Then empty intense winter sky.
Dark crouches against the walls of buildings.
The ground sinks under it.
Pale flat lemon sky,
the trees all hooks scratching.

If I could soar I could
prolong daylight on my face.
I could float on the stark
wooden light, levitating
like dried milkweed silk.

Only December and already
my bones beg for sun.
Storms have gnawed the beach
to the cliffs' base. Oaks
in the salty blast clutch ragged
brown leaves, a derelict's
paperbag of sad possessions.

Like the gulls that cross from sea to bay
at sunset screaming, I am hungry.
Among sodden leaves and hay-colored needles
I scavenge for the eye's least
nibble of green.

The market economy

Suppose some peddler offered
you can have a color TV
but your baby will be
born with a crooked spine;
you can have polyvinyl cups
and wash and wear
suits but it will cost
you your left lung
rotted with cancer; suppose
somebody offered you
a frozen precooked dinner
every night for ten years
but at the end
your colon dies
and then you do,
slowly and with much pain.
You get a house in the suburbs
but you work in a new plastics
factory and die at fifty-one
when your kidneys turn off.

But where else will you
work? where else can
you rent but Smog City?
The only houses for sale
are under the yellow sky.
You've been out of work for
a year and they're hiring
at the plastics factory.
Don't read the fine
print, there isn't any.

Martha as the angel Gabriel

for Martha Shelley

Good Martha
you back into town like a tug
small yet massive, hooting, thumping
butting and steering through
the shoals, the temptations, the rocks.
Your politics like a good engine
rattles the decks and churns the wake lively.

Sweet Martha
bulldog butterfly, koala
bear among the eucalyptus
of the Oakland hills,
your heart is shy and your
eyes dart like swallows.

Bereft Martha,
bleeding losses, you are all
you have ever loved in woman after
woman, you yourself, and in your belly
you carry your dead mother,
a pearl of an egg
with a small wet embryo bird
folded inside dreaming of wings.

You are those wings, Martha,
and in you your mother
and your mother's mother climb
to the synagogue roof, standing there
black against the sun flapping,

flapping, and take off heavily
as albatrosses, running
to lurch, lumber into the dirty air
and hang unlikely as a boot.
Then off, the big wings
hinging gracefully, higher.
For months at a time, Martha,
for years the albatross
sails the ocean winds and never
bothers to touch land
except to mate.

The love of lettuce

With a pale green curly
lust I gloat over it nestled
there on the wet earth
(oakleaf, buttercrunch, ruby, cos)
like so many nests
waiting for birds
who lay hard boiled eggs.

The first green eyes
of the mustard, the frail
wands of carrots, the fat
thrust of the peas : all
are precious as I kneel
in the mud weeding
and the thinnings go into the salad.

The garden with crooked
wandering rows dug
by the three of us
drunk with sunshine has
an intricate pattern emerging
like the back of a rug.
The tender seedlings

raise their pinheads
with the cap of seed stuck on.
Cruel and smiling with sharp
teeth is the love of lettuce.
You grow out of last year's
composted dinner and you
will end in my hot mouth.

Snow in May

It isn't supposed to happen:
snow on the apple boughs
beside the blossoms, the hills
green and white at once.
Backs steaming, horses
stand in the crusted pasture
switching their tails
in the snow, their broad
flanks like doors of leather
ovens. We lie on a mattress
in the high room with no
heat. Your body chills.
I keep taking parts of you
into my mouth, finny nose,
ears like question marks,
fatfaced toes, raspberry
cock, currant nipples, plum
balls. The snow hangs
sheets over the windows.

My grandmother used to drink
tea holding a sugar cube
between her teeth: hot boiling
strong black tea
from a glass. A gleaming
silver spoon stood up.
Before we make a fire of
our bodies I braid my black
hair and I am Grandmother braiding
her greystreaked chestnut hair
rippling to her waist before
she got into bed with me
to sleep, dead now
half my life. Ice on the palm
of my hand melting,
so cold it burns me.

The window of the woman burning

Woman dancing with hair
on fire, woman writhing in the
cone of orange snakes, flowering
into crackling lithe vines:
Woman
you are not the bound witch
at the stake, whose broiled alive
agonized screams
thrust from charred flesh
darkened Europe in the nine millions.
Woman
you are not the madonna impaled
whose sacrifice of self leaves her
empty and mad as wind,
or whore crucified
studded with nails.

Woman
you are the demon of a fountain of energy
rushing up from the coal hard
memories in the ancient spine,
flickering lights from the furnace in the solar
plexus, lush scents from the reptilian brain,
river that winds up the hypothalamus
with its fibroids of pleasure and pain
twisted and braided like rope,
firing the lanterns of the forebrain
till they glow blood red.

You are the fire sprite
that charges leaping thighs,
that whips the supple back on its arc
as deer leap through the ankles:

dance of a woman strong
in beauty that crouches
inside like a cougar in the belly
not in the eyes of others measuring.

You are the icon of woman sexual
in herself like a great forest tree
in flower, liriodendron bearing sweet tulips,
cups of joy and drunkenness.
You drink strength from your dark fierce roots
and you hang at the sun's own fiery breast
and with the green cities of your boughs
you shelter and celebrate
woman, with the cauldrons of your energies
burning red, burning green.

Going in

Every day alone whittles me.
I go to bed unmated and wake
with a vulture perched on my chest.

I suck my solitude
like a marrowbone, nothing
left but a memory of feasts.

Wait in the silence, wait
empty as a cracked eggshell
for the beating of heavy fast wings,

the soft pad of the big cat,
the dry grate of scales sliding over rock,
the boiling of the waves as It breaches.

I wait for the repressed, the unnamed,
the familiar twisted masks of early
terrors, or what I have always really known

lurks behind the door at night groping
from the corner of my eye, what breaks
through the paper hoop of sleep.

When all of my loves fall from me
like clothing, like the sweet flesh, what
stands but the bones of my childhood

ringed like a treetrunk with hunger
and glut, the tortured gaping
grin of my adolescence homely

as death. Then my bones drop away
like petals, my bones wither
and scatter and still I am waiting

empty as a grey arching sky, waiting
till I fall headlong into my center
the great roaring fiery heart

the crackling golden furnace of the sun.

Athena in the front lines

Only accidents preserve.
Athena Promachos, warrior goddess thirty feet tall,
no longer exists. Phidias
made her between wars in ruins
of a fort that had not kept the enemy out.
Making is an attack too, on bronze, on air, on time.
Sailors out on the Argo-Saronic
of gull and dolphin and bone-dry island
could see the sunlight creaking on her helmet.
A thousand years she stood over fire and mud,
then hauled as booty to Constantinople,
where the Crusaders, bouncy legionnaires
on the town, melted her down for coins.

These words are pebbles
sucked from mouth to mouth since Chaucer.
I don't believe the Etruscans or the Mayans
lacked poets, only victories.
Manuscripts under glass, women's quilts packed away
lie in the attics of museums sealed from the streets
where the tactical police are clubbing the welfare mothers.
There are no cameras, so it is not real.

Wring the stones of the hillside
for the lost plays of Sophocles they heard.
Art is nonaccident. Like love, it is
a willed tension up through the mind
balancing thrust and inertia, energy
stored in a bulb. Then the golden
trumpet of the narcissus pokes up
willfully into the sun, focusing the world.

The epigraphs stabbed the Song of Songs
through the smoking heart (The Church
Prepares for Her Bridegroom). The seven hundred thousand
four hundred fifty second tourist stared

the Venus de Milo into a brassiere ad.
Generations of women wrote poems and hid
them in drawers, because an able
woman is a bad woman. They expired
leaking radioactivity among pastel underwear.

A woman scribbling for no one doodles,
dabbles in madness, dribbles shame.
Art requires a plaza in the mind, a space
lit by the sun of regard. That tension
between maker and audience, that feedback,
that force field of interest, sustains
an I less guilty than Ego, who can utter
the truths of vision and nightmare,
the truths that spill like raw egg from the
cracking of body on body, the thousand
soft and slimy names of death, the songs
of the blind fish that swim
the caverns of bone, the songs
of the hawks who soar and stoop grappling
and screaming through the crystalline
skies of the forehead.

Though the cod stifle in the seas, though
the rivers thicken to shit, still
writing implies faith in someone listening,
different in content but not in need
from the child who cries in the night.

Making is an attack on dying, on chaos,
on blind inertia, on the second law
of thermodynamics, on indifference, on cold,
on contempt, on the silence
that does not follow the chord resolved,
the sentence spoken, but the something
that cannot be said. Perhaps there are no

words yet, perhaps the words bend the thought
back on itself, perhaps the words can be said
but cannot yet be heard, and so
the saying arches through the air and crumbles.

Making is an act, but survival
is luck, caught in history
like a moth trapped in the subway.
There is nothing to do but make well,
finish, and let go. Words
live, words die
in the mouths of everybody.

The root canal

You see before you an icing of skin,
a scum of flesh
narrowly wrapped around a tooth.
This tooth is red as a lion's
heart and it throbs.
This tooth is hollowed out to a cave
big enough for tourists
to go through in parties with guides
in flat-bottomed boats.
This tooth sings opera all night
like a Russian basso profundo.
This tooth plays itself like an organ
in an old movie palace; it is
the chief villain, Sydney Greenstreet,
and its laughter tickles with menace.
This tooth is dying, dying
like a cruel pharaoh, like a
fat gouty old tyrant assembling
his wives and his cabinet, his horse
and his generals, his dancing girls
and his hunting cheetah, all
to be burned on his tomb
in homage. I am nothing,
nothing at all, but a reluctant
pyramid standing here, a grandiose
talking headstone for my tooth.

Doors in the wind and the water

Doors open in the mind
and close again like wounds
healing. Doors open in the
mind and close again like
dying fish whose gills fall
finally still. Doors in the mind
open and close like mountains
you see spired white past other
mountains but never reach.

Doors open flashing in the sundarkened wave,
doors in the brown carp pool,
doors in the beard of the waterfall,
doors in the green caverns
of the tree, doors in the eye
of the goat, of the alley cat,
doors in a hand held up,
doors in the astonished skin.

The self is last summer's
clothes unpacked from suitcases.
The self is your old physics
notebook filled with experiments
you had to fake. A well thumbed
deck where the joker fills in
for the King of Diamonds

and the dog has eaten the Ace
of Spades, but there are
five battered sevens.

Always too at the root tips growing
or dying, dark osmotic exchange
of particles, of energy, of dreams
goes wetly on. The larger mysteries
come to us at morning and evening
crowned with bladderwrack and gull feathers,
wearing the heads of cows, of horned owls,
of our children who are not ours,
of strangers whose faces open
like doors where we enter
or flee.

You ask why sometimes I say stop

You ask why sometimes I say stop
why sometimes I cry no
while I shake with pleasure.
What do I fear, you ask,
why don't I always want to come
and come again to that molten
deep sea center where the nerves
fuse open and the brain
and body shine with a black wordless light
fluorescent and heaving like plankton.

If you turn over the old refuse
of sexual slang, the worn buttons
of language, you find men
talk of spending and women
of dying.

You come in a torrent and ease
into limpness. Pleasure takes me
farther and farther from shore
in a series of breakers, each
towering higher before it
crashes and spills flat.

I am open then as a palm held out,
open as a sunflower, without

crust, without shelter, without
skin, hideless and unhidden.
How can I let you ride
so far into me and not fear?

Helpless as a burning city,
how can I ignore that the extremes
of pleasure are fire storms
that leave a vacuum into which
dangerous feelings (tenderness,
affection, l o v e) may rush
like gale force winds.

Smalley Bar

Anchored a ways off Buoy Rocks the sailboat
bobs jaunty, light, little. We slide
over the side after scraping bottom.
The water up to our waists looks brown
ahead. We wade onto Smalley Bar.
I leave the men clamming and walk
the bar toward shore.

By the time I walk back straight out
from the coast of the wild island the tide
is rushing in. My shoes already float.
I walk the bar, invisible now,
water to my thighs. The day's
turned smoky. A storm is blowing
thick from the east. I stand
a quarter mile out in the bay with
the tide rising and only this
strange buried bridge of sandbar under me,
calling across the breaking grey waves,
unsure whether I can still wade
or must swim against the tide to the boat
dragging its anchor loose.

Unknown territory. Strange bottom.
I live on bridges that may or may
not be there under the breaking
water deepening. I never know
what I'll step on. I never know
whether I'll make it before dark,
before the storm catches me,

214

before the tide sweeps me out.
The neat white houses across the bay
are fading as the air thickens.
People in couples, in boxes, in clear
expectations of class and role
and income, I deserve no pity
shivering here as the water rushes past.
I find more than clams out on
the bar. It's not my sailboat
ever, but it's my choice.

For Shoshana Rihn—Pat Swinton

History falls like rain
on the fields, like hailstones
that break the graceful
fleur de lis spears
of young corn. History falls
like freezing rain
on the small hopes, the
small pleasures of the morning,
the small struggles of a life.
History falls like bombs
scorching the birds on their nests,
burning the big-eyed voles in their tunnels,
the rabbits giving suck
curled in the green grass of June.
Craters pit the smoking fields.
A right hand, a left foot
scattered on the broken road.

History is manufactured like
plastic buckets. History is traded
on the stock exchange and the big
holding corporations
rake off a profit.
History is written to order
like the Sunday funnies. History
is floated like a bond issue
on the fat of banks.

Sometimes time funnels down
to the dripping of water
one drop at a time slow
as the slowest tears right
on the forehead of someone lying
awake remembering, remembering
another year and another face.
Sometimes time stalls in a door

opening, a moment balanced
on a blade of choice when the hand
falters, the face freezes,
and then finally the doors of the will
open or shut
on a yes or a no.

Beyond official history of texts,
of bronze generals,
a history flows of rivers and amoebas,
of the first creeping thing
that shuddered onto the land,
a history of the woman who
tamed corn, a history
of learning and losing, a history
of making good and being had,
of some great green organism
gasping to be free.

Sometimes time funnels down
to a woman who stands in a door
saying no to those who come
with guns and warrants.
Sometimes silence
is a song that carries on the soiled wind
like a flight of geese winging north
to clear cold waters. Sometimes
history that matters is seizing your own,
the old blood clots, the too short dresses,
the anguished masks of failures half
remembered like childhood fevers,
matchboxes from motels off freeways,
snapshots with faces torn out, letters
that said too much or too little,
and saying yes. Yes, I am the person
who acted, who spoke. I grow

from what I was
like a pitch pine after a fire
that pokes up green and bushy shoots
from the charred ground
where its roots spread deep and wide.
I grow from what I was,
more, not less, yes,
in me both egg and stone.
No, I am not a soldier in your
history, I live in my own tale
with others I choose to wake me in the morning,
to sit across the table in the evening,
to wipe my forehead, to touch
my hand, to carry in my throat
like a lullaby that murmurs
no, I do not fear you
and yes, I am not for sale.

In the wet

How you shine from the inside
orange as a pumpkin's belly,
your face beautiful as children's
faces when they want
at white heat, when fear pinches
them, when they have not learned
how to lie well
yet.

Your pain flows into me through
my ears and fingers. Your pain
presses in, I cannot keep it away.
Like a baby in my body
you kick me as you stretch
and knock the breath out.

Yet when I shook with pain's
fever, when fear chewed me
raw all night, you held me, you
held on. Then I was the baby
past words and blubbering.
The words, the comfort were yours
and you nurtured me shriveled
like a seed that would
never uncurl.

How strangely we mother each
other, sister and brother, lovers,
twins. For you to love me means
you must love yourself.
That is what loving is, I say,
it is not pain, it is not
pleasure, it is not compulsion
or fantasy. It is only a way
of living, wide open.

Crows

They give me a bad
reputation, those swart rowers
through the air, heavy winged
and heavy voiced, brass tipped.
Before us they lived here
in the tallest pine. Shortly
after coming I walked in
on a ceremony, the crows
were singing secretly
and beautifully a ritual.
They divebombed me. To make
peace I brought a sacrifice,
the remains of a leg
of lamb. Since then
we have had truce.
Smart, ancient, rowdy and far-
sighted, they use our land
as sanctuary for raiding
where men shoot at them.

They come down, settling like
unwieldy cargo jets, to the bird
food, scattering the
cardinals, the juncos. *God
they're big, I've never seen
them so near a house,*
the guest says. We look
at each other, the crows
and me. Outside
they allow my slow approach.
They do not touch our crops

even in the far garden
in the bottomland. I'm aware
women have been burned
for less. I stand
under the oldest white oak
whose arms coil fat as pythons
and scream at the hunters
driving them back
with black hair coarse and streaming:
Caw! Caw!

If they come in the night

Long ago on a night of danger and vigil
a friend said, *Why are you happy?*
He explained (we lay together
on a hard cold floor) what prison
meant because he had done
time, and I talked of the death
of friends. *Why are you happy
then,* he asked, close to
angry.

I said, I like my life. If I
have to give it back, if they
take it from me, let me only
not feel I wasted any, let me
not feel I forgot to love anyone
I meant to love, that I forgot
to give what I held in my hands,
that I forgot to do some little
piece of the work that wanted
to come through.

Sun and moonshine, starshine,
the muted grey light off the waters
of the bay at night, the white
light of the fog stealing in,
the first spears of the morning
touching a face
I love. We all lose
everything. We lose
ourselves. We are lost.

Only what we manage to do
lasts, what love sculps from us;

but what I count, my rubies, my
children, are those moments
wide open when I know clearly
who I am, who you are, what we
do, a marigold, an oakleaf, a meteor,
with all my senses hungry and filled
at once like a pitcher with light.

At the core

Quiet setting the rough hairy roots
into the hole, tamping the compost;
quiet cutting the chicken between
the bones, so the knife
rarely needs sharpening as it
senses the way through;
quiet in the hollow setting
the feet down carefully so the quail
bow their heads and go on pecking;
silence as my cats walk round
and round me in bed butting
and kneading my chest with their
sharp morning feet;
silence of body on body until
the knot of the self loosens gushing;
my living is words placed end to end,
oddly assorted cuneiform bricks
half broken, crumbling, sharp,
just baked with shiny sides
and raw edges. Even in sleep
words clatter through my head
roughly, like a wheelbarrow of
bricks dumped out. Words are my work,
my tools, my weapons, my follies,
my posterity, my faith.
Yet when I grasp myself I find
the coarse black hair
and warm slowly heaving flank
of silence digging with strong
nailed feet its burrow
in the tongueless earth.

Beauty I would suffer for

Last week a doctor told me
anemic after an operation
to eat: ordered to indulgence,
given a papal dispensation to run
amok in Zabar's.
Yet I know that in
two weeks, a month I
will have in my nostrils
not the savor of roasting goose,
not the burnt sugar of caramel topping
the Saint-Honoré cake, not the pumpernickel
bearing up the sweet butter, the sturgeon
but again the scorched wire,
burnt rubber smell
of willpower, living
with the brakes on.

I want to pass into the boudoirs
of Rubens' women. I want to dance
graceful in my tonnage like Poussin nymphs.
Those melon bellies, those vast ripening thighs,
those featherbeds of forearms, those buttocks
placid and gross as hippopotami:
how I would bend myself
to that standard of beauty, how faithfully
I would consume waffles and sausage for breakfast
with croissants on the side, how dutifully
I would eat for supper the blackbean soup
with Madeira, followed by the fish course,
the meat course, and the Bavarian cream.
Even at intervals during the day I would
suffer an occasional éclair
for the sake of appearance.

A gift of light

Grape conserve from the red Caco vine
planted five years ago:
rooted deep in the good dark loam
of the bottomland, where centuries
have washed the topsoil from the sandy
hill of pine and oak, whose bark
shows the scabs of fire.
Once this was an orchard on a farm.
When lilacs bloom in May I can find
the cellar hole of the old house.
Once this was a village of Pamet Indians.
From shell middens I can find their campground.

From the locust outside my window the fierce
hasty October winds have stripped the delicate
grassgreen fingernails. Winter is coming early.
The birds that go are gone, the plants retreating
underground, their hope in tubers, bulb and seed.

The peaches, the tomatoes, the pears
glow like muted lanterns on their shelves. All
is put down for the winter except the root crops
still tunneling under the salt hay mulch
we gathered at the mouth of the Herring River
as the sun kippered our salty brown backs.
Even the fog that day was hot as soup.
At evening when we made love
our skin tasted of tears and leather.

This year the autumn colors are muted. Too
much rain, the winds tore the leaves loose
before they cured. I braid my life in its
strong and muted colors and I taste my love
in me this morning like something harsh

and sweet, like raw sugarcane I chewed in Cuba,
fresh cut, oozing sap.

On those Washington avenues that resemble
emperor-sized cemeteries, vast Roman mausoleum
after mausoleum where Justice and Health
are budgeted out of existence for the many,
men who smell of good cologne are pushing pins
across maps. It is time to attack the left
again, it is time for a mopping up
operation against those of us who opposed
their wars too soon, too seriously, too long.
It is time to silence the shrill voices
of women whose demands incommode men
with harems of illpaid secretaries, men
for whom industries purr, men who buy death wholesale.
Today some are released from prison and others
are sucked in. Those who would not talk
to grand juries are boxed from the light
to grow fungus on their brains and those
who talked receive a message it is time
to talk again.

I try hard to be simple, to remember always
to ask for whom what is done is done.
Who gets and who loses? Who pays
and who rakes off the profit? Whose
life is shortened? Whose heat
is shut off? Whose children end
shooting up or shot in the streets?

I try to remember to ask simple questions,
I try to remember to love my friends and fight
my enemies. But their faces are hidden
in the vaults of banks, their names are inscribed

on the great plains by strip mining and you can
only read the script from Mars. Their secret
wills are encoded in the computers that mind
nuclear submarines armed with the godheads
of death. They enter me in the drugs I buy
that erode my genes. They enter my blood invisible
as the Sevin in the water that flows
from the tap, as strontium 90 in milk.

You are part comrade and part enemy; you
are part guerrilla and part prison guard. Sometimes
you care more to control me than for winning
this lifelong war. If I am your colony
you differ only in scale from Rockefeller.
I want to trust you the way I want
to drink water when my tongue is parched
and blistered, the way I want to crouch
by a fire when I have hiked miles
through the snowy woods and my toes are numb.

Let no one doubt, no onlookers, no heirs
of our agonies, how much I have loved
what I have loved. Flying back
from Washington, I saw the air steely
bright out to the huge bell of horizon.
I leaned against the plane window, cheek
to the plastic, crooning to see the curve
of the Cape hooking out in the embrace
of the water, to see the bays, the tidal
rivers, the intricate web of marshes,
the whole body of this land like beautiful

lace, like a fraying bronze net laid
on the glittering fish belly of the sea.

I sink my hands into this hillside wrist
deep. My nails are stubby and under them
always is my own land's dirt. I bring you
this gift of grape conserve from shelves
of summer sun bottled like glowing lights
I hope we will survive free and contentious to taste,
as I bring myself, my mouth opening
to taste you, my hands that know how
to touch you, belly and back and cunt,
history and politics. I bring you trouble
like a hornet's nest in a hat
to roost on your head. I bring you
struggle and trouble and love
and a gift of grape conserve to melt
on your tongue, red and winy,
the summer sun within like soft jewels
passing and strong and sweet.

The inside chance

Dance like a jackrabbit
in the dunegrass, dance
not for release, no
the ice holds hard but
for the promise. Yesterday
the chickadees sang *fever*,
fever, the mating song.
You can still cross ponds
leaving tracks in the snow
over the sleeping fish
but in the marsh the red
maples look red
again, their buds swelling.
Just one week ago a blizzard
roared for two days.
Ice weeps in the road.
Yet spring hides
in the snow. On the south
wall of the house
the first sharp crown
of crocus sticks out.
Spring lurks inside the hard
casing, and the bud
begins to crack. What seems
dead pares its hunger
sharp and stirs groaning.
If we have not stopped
wanting in the long dark,
we will grasp our desires
soon by the nape.
Inside the fallen brown
apple the seed is alive.
Freeze and thaw, freeze
and thaw, the sap leaps

in the maple under the bark
and although they have
pronounced us dead, we
rise again invisibly,
we rise and the sun sings
in us sweet and smoky
as the blood of the maple
that will open its leaves
like thousands of waving hands.

Night flight

Vol de nuit : It's that French
phrase comes to me out of a dead
era, a closet where the bones of pets
and dried jellyfish are stored. Dreams
of a twenty-year-old are salty water
and the residual stickiness of berry jam
but they have the power to paralyze
a swimmer out beyond her depth and strength.
Memory's a minefield.

Saint Exupéry was a favorite of my French
former husband. Every love has its
season, its cultural artifacts, shreds
of popular song like a billboard
peeling in strips to the faces behind,
endearments and scents, patchouli,
musk, cabbage, vanilla, male cat, smoked
herring. Yet I call this cobalt and crystal
outing, vol de nuit.

Alone in a row on the half empty late
plane I sit by the window holding myself.
As the engines roar and the plane quivers
and then bursts forward I am tensed
and tuned for the high arc of flight
between snowfields, frozen lakes and the cold
distant fires of the clustered stars. Below
the lights of cities burn like fallen galaxies,
ordered, radial, pulsing.

Sometimes hurtling down a highway through
the narrow cone of headlights I feel
moments of exaltation, but my night
vision is poor. I pretend at control

as I drive, nervously edging that knowledge
I am not really managing. I am in the hands
of strangers and of luck. By flight *he* meant
flying and I mean being flown, totally
beyond volition, willfully.

We fall in love with strangers whose faces
radiate a familiar power that reminds us
of something lost before we had it.
The braille of the studious fingers instructs
exactly what we have succumbed to, far too late
to close, to retract the self that has extruded
from us naked, vulnerable and sticky,
the foot, the tentative eyestalked head
of the mating snail.

To fall in love so late is dangerous. Below,
lights are winking out. Cars crawl into driveways
and fade into the snow. Planes make me think
of dying suddenly, and loving of dying
slowly, the heat loss of failure and betrayed
trust. Yet I cast myself on you, closing
my eyes as I leap and then opening them wide
as I land. Love is plunging into darkness toward
a place that may exist.

Excursions, incursions

1.

"Learning to manage the process
of technological innovation
more productively" is the theme
of the speech the man beside me
on the plane to Washington
will be saying to a Congressional
subcommittee. He works at M.I.T.
He drinks a martini, glancing sideways.
His watch flashes numbers; it houses
a tiny computer. He observes
me in snatches, data to analyze:
the two-piece V-neck dress
from New York, the manuscript
I am cutting, the wild black
hair, the dirt under my stubby nails.
It doesn't scan. I pretend
I do not see him looking
while I try to read his speech,
pretending not to: a neutron
bomb of deadly language that kills
all warm-blooded creatures
but leaves the system standing.
He rates my face and body at-
tractive but the presence
disturbing. Chop, chop, I want
to say, sure, we are enemies.
Watch out. I try to decide
if I can learn anything useful
to my side if I let him
engage me in a game of
conversation.

2.

At the big round table in the university
club, the faculty are chatting
about wives, marriages, divorces, visiting
arrangements. They all belong
to the same kinship system. They have
one partner at a time, then terminate.
Monogamy means that the husband has
sex only a couple of times with each
other female, I figure out, and
the wife, only with him. Afterwards
the children spend summers/weekends/
Sundays with the father.

Listening becomes eavesdropping and they
begin to feel my silence like a horse
in the diningroom. Gradually as I sit
my hair mats. Feathers stick up from
it, crow and eagle. My cheeks break
out into painted zigzag designs. My spear
leans against the back of my chair.
They begin to question me, oh, um,
do you live communally? What do
you mean, "open"? Hair breaks through
the back of my hands. My fangs
drum on the table top. In another moment
I will swing by my long prehensile
tail from the crystal chandelier,
shitting in the soup.

3.

The men are laughing as I approach
and then they price me: that calculating

scan. Everything turns into hornets
buzzing, swarming. One will
tell me about his wife
weeping tears of pure beersuds;
one is even now swaggering down
the Tombstone set of his mind, the fastest
gun; one will let me know in the next
half hour he thinks political writers
are opportunistic simpletons, and women
have minds of goat fudge; one will
only try unceasingly to bed me as if
I were the week's prize, and he wears
a chain of fellowships and grants
like sharpshooters' medals. Mostly they
will chase the students and drink, mostly
they will gossip and put each other
down, mostly they will complain. I
am here for the women, a political
task. They think they have a label
for that. I am on vacation from sex
and love, from the fatty broth
of my life. I am seeking to be useful,
the good godmother. We are acting
in different fables. I know the plots
of theirs, but none of them recognize
mine, except the students, who understand
at once they will be allowed
to chew me to the bones.

4.

I am sitting on a kitchen chair.
My feet do not reach the floor.
If I sit forward, they'll rest on
a rung, but if I do that, the women

will stop talking and look at me
and I'll be made to go outside
and "play" in this taffeta dress.
What they say is not what they
are talking about, which lumps
just underneath. If I listen, if I
screw up my face and hold my breath
and listen, I'll see it, the moving
bump under the rug, that snake in the
tablecloth jungle, the bulge
in women's dresses you aren't supposed
to notice. I listen and listen
but it doesn't go anyplace,
nobody comes out all
right in the end. I get bored
and kick the table leg and am sent
outside to sulk, still not knowing.

I never got there, into the hot
wet heart of the kitchen gossip,
to sit twisting the ring on my finger
worn smooth, saying my hubby, my old
man, *him*. I never grew up, Mama,
I grew off, I grew outside. I grew
like crazy. I am the calico
mouse gnawing at the foundations.
The sweet snake is my friend who chews
on the roots of the hangman's tree
to bring it down. I am the lump
under the tablecloth that moves
stealthily toward the cream pitcher.
After years under the rug like a tumor
they invite me into the parlor, Mama,
they pay me by check and it doesn't bounce.
I'm giving a speech tonight. Do they
think I'm kidding? The walls I write

240

on are for sale now, but the message
is the same as I wrote in
blood on the jail house wall.
Energy flowing through me gets turned
into money and they take that back,
but the work remains, Mama, under
the carpet, in the walls, out
in the open. It goes on talking
after they've shut me up.

Apologies

Moments
when I care about nothing
except an apple:
red as a maple tree
satin and speckled
tart and winy.

Moments
when body is all:
fast as an elevator
pulsing out waves of darkness
hot as the inner earth
molten and greedy.

Moments
when sky fills my head:
bluer than thought
cleaner than number
with a wind
fresh and sour
cold from the mouth of the sea.

Moments
of sinking my teeth
into now like a hungry fox:
never otherwise
am I so cruel;
never otherwise
so happy.

The long death

for Wendy Teresa Simon
(September 25, 1954–August 7, 1979)

Radiation is like oppression,
the average daily kind of subliminal toothache
you get almost used to, the stench
of chlorine in the water, of smog in the wind.

We comprehend the disasters of the moment,
the nursing home fire, the river in flood
pouring over the sandbag levee, the airplane
crash with fragments of burnt bodies
scattered among the hunks of twisted metal,
the grenade in the marketplace, the sinking ship.

But how to grasp a thing that does not
kill you today or tomorrow
but slowly from the inside in twenty years.
How to feel that a corporate choice
means we bear twisted genes and our
grandchildren will be stillborn if our
children are very lucky.

Slow death can not be photographed for the six
o'clock news. It's all statistical,
the gross national product or the prime
lending rate. Yet if our eyes saw
in the right spectrum, how it would shine,
lurid as magenta neon.

If we could smell radiation like seeping
gas, if we could sense it as heat, if we
could hear it as a low ominous roar
of the earth shifting, then we would not sit
and be poisoned while industry spokesmen
talk of acceptable millirems and .02
cancer per population thousand.

We acquiesce at murder so long as it is slow,
murder from asbestos dust, from tobacco,
from lead in the water, from sulphur in the air,
and fourteen years later statistics are printed
on the rise in leukemia among children.
We never see their faces. They never stand,
those poisoned children together in a courtyard,
and are gunned down by men in three-piece suits.

The shipyard workers who built nuclear
submarines, the soldiers who were marched
into the Nevada desert to be tested by the H-
bomb, the people who work in power plants,
they die quietly years after in hospital
wards and not on the evening news.

The soft spring rain floats down and the air
is perfumed with pine and earth. Seedlings
drink it in, robins sip it in puddles,
you run in it and feel clean and strong,
the spring rain blowing from the irradiated
cloud over the power plant.

Radiation is oppression, the daily average
kind, the kind you're almost used to
and live with as the years abrade you,
high blood pressure, ulcers, cramps, migraine,
a hacking cough : you take it inside
and it becomes pain and you say, not
They are killing me, but *I am sick now.*

The cast off

This is a day to celebrate can-
openers, those lantern-jawed long-tailed
humping tools that cut through what keeps
us from what we need: a can of beans
trapped in its armor taunts the nails
and teeth of a hungry woman.

Today let us hear hurrahs for zippers,
those small shark teeth that part
politely to let us at what we want;
the tape on packages that unlock
us birthday presents; envelopes
we slit to thaw the frozen
words on the tundra of paper.

Today let us praise the small
rebirths, the emerging groundhog
from the sodden burrow; the nut
picked from the broken fortress of walnut
shell, itself pried from the oily fruit
shaken from the high turreted
city of the tree.

Today let us honor the safe whose door
hangs ajar; the champagne bottle
with its cork bounced off the ceiling
and into the soup tureen; the Victorian lady
in love who has removed her hood, her cloak,
her laced boots, her stockings, her overdress,

her underdress, her wool petticoat, her linen
petticoats, her silk petticoats, her whalebone
corset, her bustle, her chemise, her drawers, and
who still wants to! Today let us praise the cast
that finally opens, slit neatly in two
like a dinosaur egg, and out at last
comes somewhat hairier, powdered in dead skin
but still beautiful, the lost for months
body of my love.

Rainy 4th

I am someone who boots myself from bed
when the alarm cracks my sleep. Spineless
as raw egg on the tilted slab of day
I ooze toward breakfast to be born.
I stagger to my desk on crutches of strong coffee.

How sensuous then are the mornings we do
not rise. This morning we curl embracing
while rain crawls over the roof like a thousand
scuttling fiddler crabs. Set off a
twenty-one tea kettle salute
for a rainy 4th with the parade and races
cancelled, our picnic chilling disconsolate
in five refrigerators. A sneaky hooray
for the uneven gallop of the drops,
for the steady splash of the drainpipe,
for the rushing of the leaves in green
whooshing wet bellows, for the teeming wind
that blows the house before it in full sail.

We are at sea together in the woods.
The air chill enough for the quilt, warm
and sweet as cocoa and coconut we make
love in the morning when there's never time.
Now time rains over us liquid and vast.
We talk facing, elastic parentheses.
We dawdle in green mazes of conversing
seeking no way out but only farther into
the undulating hedges, grey statues of nymphs,
satyrs and learned old women, broken busts,
past a fountain and tombstone
in the boxwood of our curious minds
that like the pole beans on the fence
expand perceptibly in the long rain.

247

Attack of the squash people

And thus the people every year
in the valley of humid July
did sacrifice themselves
to the long green phallic god
and eat and eat and eat.

They're coming, they're on us,
the long striped gourds, the silky
babies, the hairy adolescents,
the lumpy vast adults
like the trunks of green elephants.
Recite fifty zucchini recipes!

Zucchini tempura; creamed soup;
sauté with olive oil and cumin,
tomatoes, onion; frittata;
casserole of lamb; baked
topped with cheese; marinated;
stuffed; stewed; driven
through the heart like a stake.

Get rid of old friends: they too
have gardens and full trunks.
Look for newcomers: befriend
them in the post office, unload
on them and run. Stop tourists
in the street. Take truckloads

to Boston. Give to your Red Cross.
Beg on the highway: please
take my zucchini, I have a crippled
mother at home with heartburn.

Sneak out before dawn to drop
them in other people's gardens,
in baby buggies at churchdoors.
Shot, smuggling zucchini into
mailboxes, a federal offense.

With a suave reptilian glitter
you bask among your raspy
fronds sudden and huge as
alligators. You give and give
too much, like summer days
limp with heat, thunderstorms
bursting their bags on our heads,
as we salt and freeze and pickle
for the too little to come.

Intruding

What are you doing up, my cat
complains as I come into the living
room at two in the morning: she
is making eyes through the glass
at a squat ruffed grey tom. He fades
back, only the gold eyes shining
like headlights under the bird feeder.

Retreat with all deliberate speed
says the skunk in the path
at the marsh's edge, tail upraised
quivering in shape like a question
mark but in meaning an exclamation
point.

You are too near my nest so I will
let you believe you can catch and
eat me, says the whip-poor-will
leading me through the thorniest thickets
uphill and down ravines of briar
as it drags its apparently broken wing.

This is my lair, my home, my master,
my piss-post, my good brown blanket,
my feeding dish, my bone farm, all
mine and my teeth are long and sharp
as icicles and my tongue is red as your
blood I will spill if you do not
run, the German shepherd says loudly
and for half a block.

In the center of her web the spider
crouches to charge me. In the woods
the blue jay shrieks and the squirrels

perch over my head chittering while all
the small birds bide silent in the leaves.
Wherever I march on two legs
I am walking on somebody's roof.

But when I sit still and alone
trees hatch warblers rapid as sparks.
The price of seeing is silence.
A voracious furnace of shrew darts
in the grass like a truncated snake.
On my arm a woodnymph lights probing
me curiously, faintly, as she opens
and closes the tapestried doors of flight.

September afternoon
at four o'clock

Full in the hand, heavy
with ripeness, perfume spreading
its fan : moments now resemble
sweet russet pears glowing
on the bough, peaches warm
from the afternoon sun, amber
and juicy, flesh that can
make you drunk.

There is a turn in things
that makes the heart catch.
We are ripening, all the hard
green grasping, the stony will
swelling into sweetness, the acid
and sugar in balance, the sun
stored as energy that is pleasure
and pleasure that is energy.

Whatever happens, whatever,
we say, and hold hard and let
go and go on. In the perfect
moment the future coils,
a tree inside a pit. Take,
eat, we are each other's
perfection, the wine of our
mouths is sweet and heavy.
Soon enough comes the vinegar.
The fruit is ripe for the taking
and we take. There is
no other wisdom.

Morning athletes

for Gloria Nardin Watts

Most mornings we go running side by side
two women in mid-lives jogging, awkward
in our baggy improvisations, two
bundles of rejects from the thrift shop.
Men in their zippy outfits run in packs
on the road where we park, meet
like lovers on the wood's edge and walk
sedately around the corner out of sight
to our own hardened clay road, High Toss.

Slowly we shuffle, serious, panting
but talking as we trot, our old honorable
wounds in knee and back and ankle paining
us, short, fleshy, dark haired, Italian
and Jew, with our full breasts carefully
confined. We are rich earthy cooks
both of us and the flesh we are working
off was put on with grave pleasure. We
appreciate each other's cooking, each
other's art, photographer and poet, jogging
in the chill and wet and green, in the blaze
of young sun, talking over our work,
our plans, our men, our ideas, watching
each other like a pot that might boil dry
for that sign of too harsh fatigue.

It is not the running I love, thump
thump with my leaden feet that only
infrequently are winged and prancing,
but the light that glints off the cattails
as the wind furrows them, the rum cherries
reddening leaf and fruit, the way the pines
blacken the sunlight on their bristles,

the hawk circling, stooping, floating
low over beige grasses,
                    and your company
as we trot, two friendly dogs leaving
tracks in the sand. The geese call
on the river wandering lost in sedges
and we talk and pant, pant and talk
in the morning early and busy together.

Cats like angels

Cats like angels are supposed to be thin;
pigs like cherubs are supposed to be fat.
People are mostly in between, a knob
of bone sticking out in the knee you might
like to pad, a dollop of flab hanging
over the belt. You punish yourself,
one of those rubber balls kids have
that come bouncing back off their own
paddles, rebounding on the same slab.
You want to be slender and seamless
as a bolt.
       When I was a girl
I loved spiny men with ascetic grimaces
all elbows and words and cartilage
ribbed like cast up fog-grey hulls,
faces to cut the eyes blind
on the glittering blade, chins
of Aegean prows bent on piracy.

Now I look for men whose easy bellies
show a love for the flesh and the table,
men who will come in the kitchen
and sit, who don't think peeling potatoes
makes their penis shrink; men with broad
fingers and purple figgy balls,
men with rumpled furrows and the slightly
messed look at ease of beds recently
well used.
       We are not all supposed
to look like undernourished fourteen year
old boys, no matter what the fashions
ordain. You are built to pull a cart,

to lift a heavy load and bear it,
to haul up the long slope, and so
am I, peasant bodies, earthy, solid
shapely dark glazed clay pots that can
stand on the fire. When we put our
bellies together we do not clatter
but bounce on the good upholstery.

For strong women

A strong woman is a woman who is straining.
A strong woman is a woman standing
on tiptoe and lifting a barbell
while trying to sing Boris Godunov.
A strong woman is a woman at work
cleaning out the cesspool of the ages,
and while she shovels, she talks about
how she doesn't mind crying, it opens
the ducts of the eyes, and throwing up
develops the stomach muscles, and
she goes on shoveling with tears
in her nose.

A strong woman is a woman in whose head
a voice is repeating, I told you so,
ugly, bad girl, bitch, nag, shrill, witch,
ballbuster, nobody will ever love you back,
why aren't you feminine, why aren't
you soft, why aren't you quiet, why
aren't you dead?

A strong woman is a woman determined
to do something others are determined
not be done. She is pushing up on the bottom
of a lead coffin lid. She is trying to raise
a manhole cover with her head, she is trying
to butt her way through a steel wall.
Her head hurts. People waiting for the hole
to be made say, hurry, you're so strong.

A strong woman is a woman bleeding
inside. A strong woman is a woman making
herself strong every morning while her teeth
loosen and her back throbs. Every baby,
a tooth, midwives used to say, and now
every battle a scar. A strong woman

is a mass of scar tissue that aches
when it rains and wounds that bleed
when you bump them and memories that get up
in the night and pace in boots to and fro.

A strong woman is a woman who craves love
like oxygen or she turns blue choking.
A strong woman is a woman who loves
strongly and weeps strongly and is strongly
terrified and has strong needs. A strong woman is strong
in words, in action, in connection, in feeling;
she is not strong as a stone but as a wolf
suckling her young. Strength is not in her, but she
enacts it as the wind fills a sail.

What comforts her is others loving
her equally for the strength and for the weakness
from which it issues, lightning from a cloud.
Lightning stuns. In rain, the clouds disperse.
Only water of connection remains,
flowing through us. Strong is what we make
each other. Until we are all strong together,
a strong woman is a woman strongly afraid.

For the young who want to

Talent is what they say
you have after the novel
is published and favorably
reviewed. Beforehand what
you have is a tedious
delusion, a hobby like knitting.

Work is what you have done
after the play is produced
and the audience claps.
Before that friends keep asking
when you are planning to go
out and get a job.

Genius is what they know you
had after the third volume
of remarkable poems. Earlier
they accuse you of withdrawing,
ask why you don't have a baby,
call you a bum.

The reason people want M.F.A.'s,
take workshops with fancy names
when all you can really
learn is a few techniques,
typing instructions and some-
body else's mannerisms

is that every artist lacks
a license to hang on the wall

like your optician, your vet
proving you may be a clumsy sadist
whose fillings fall into the stew
but you're certified a dentist.

The real writer is one
who really writes. Talent
is an invention like phlogiston
after the fact of fire.
Work is its own cure. You have to
like it better than being loved.

Hand games

Intent gets blocked by noise.
How often what we spoke
in the bathtub, weeping
water to water, what we framed
lying flat in bed to the spiked
night is not the letter that arrives,
the letter we thought we sent. We drive
toward each other on expressways
without exits. The telephone
turns our voices into codes,
then decodes the words falsely,
terms of an equation
that never balances, a scale
forever awry with its foot
stuck up lamely like a scream.

Drinking red wine from a sieve,
trying to catch love in words,
its strong brown river in flood
pours through our weak bones.
A kitten will chase the beam of a flash
light over the floor. We learn
some precious and powerful forces
cannot be touched, and what
we touch plump and sweet
as a peach from the tree, a tomato
from the vine, sheds the name
as if we tried to write in pencil
on its warm and fragrant skin.

Mostly the television is on
and the washer is running and the kettle
shrieks it's boiling while the telephone
rings. Mostly we are worrying about

the fuel bill and how to pay the taxes
and whether the diet is working
when the moment of vulnerability
lights on the nose like a blue moth,
then flitters away. In the leaking
sieve of our bodies we carry
the blood of our love.

Right to life

SAILLE

A woman is not a pear tree
thrusting her fruit in mindless fecundity
into the world. Even pear trees bear
heavily one year and rest and grow the next.
An orchard gone wild drops few warm rotting
fruit in the grass but the trees stretch
high and wiry gifting the birds forty
feet up among inch long thorns
broken atavistically from the smooth wood.

A woman is not a basket you place
your buns in to keep them warm. Not a brood
hen you can slip duck eggs under.
Not a purse holding the coins of your
descendants till you spend them in wars.
Not a bank where your genes gather interest
and interesting mutations in the tainted
rain, any more than you are.

You plant corn and you harvest
it to eat or sell. You put the lamb
in the pasture to fatten and haul it in
to butcher for chops. You slice
the mountain in two for a road and gouge
the high plains for coal and the waters
run muddy for miles and years.
Fish die but you do not call them yours
unless you wished to eat them.

Now you legislate mineral rights in a woman.
You lay claim to her pastures for grazing,
fields for growing babies like iceberg
lettuce. You value children so dearly

that none ever go hungry, none weep
with no one to tend them when mothers
work, none lack fresh fruit,
none chew lead or cough to death and your
orphanages are empty. Every noon the best
restaurants serve poor children steaks.

At this moment at nine o'clock a *partera*
is performing a table top abortion on an
unwed mother in Texas who can't get Medicaid
any longer. In five days she will die
of tetanus and her little daughter will cry
and be taken away. Next door a husband
and wife are sticking pins in the son
they did not want. They will explain
for hours how wicked he is,
how he wants discipline.

We are all born of woman, in the rose
of the womb we suckled our mother's blood
and every baby born has a right to love
like a seedling to sun. Every baby born
unloved, unwanted is a bill that will come
due in twenty years with interest, an anger
that must find a target, a pain that will
beget pain. A decade downstream a child
screams, a woman falls, a synagogue is torched,
a firing squad is summoned, a button
is pushed and the world burns.

I will choose what enters me, what becomes
flesh of my flesh. Without choice, no politics,
no ethics lives. I am not your cornfield,

not your uranium mine, not your calf
for fattening, not your cow for milking.
You may not use me as your factory.
Priests and legislators do not hold
shares in my womb or my mind.
This is my body. If I give it to you
I want it back. My life
is a non-negotiable demand.

Shadows of the burning

D U I R

Oak burns steady and hot and long
and fires of oak are traditional tonight
but we light a fire of pitch pine
which burns well enough in the salt wind
whistling while ragged flames lick the dark
casting our shadows high as the dunes.

Come into the fire and catch,
come in, come in. Fire that burns
and leaves entire, the silver flame
of the moon, trembling mercury laying
on the waves a highway to the abyss,
the full roaring furnace of the sun at zenith
of the year and potency, midsummer's eve.

Come dance in the fire, come in.
This is the briefest night and just
under the ocean the fires of the sun
roll toward us. Already your skin is dark,
already your wiry curls are tipped with gold
and my black hair begins to redden.

How often I have leapt into that fire,
how often burned like a torch, my hair
streaming sparks, and wakened to weep
ashes. I have said, love is a downer we take,
love is a habit like sucking on death tit cigarettes,
love is a bastard art. Instead of painting
or composing, we compose a beloved.
When you love for a living, I have said,
you're doomed to early retirement without benefits.

For women have died and worms have eaten them
and just for love. Love of the wrong man or

the right. Death from abortion, from the first
child or the eighteenth, death at the stake
for loving a woman or freedom or the wrong
deity. Death at the open end of a gun
from a jealous man, a vengeful man,
Othello's fingers, Henry's ax.

It is romance I loathe, the swooning moon
of June which croons to the tune of every goon.
Venus on the half shell without the reek
of seaweed preferred to Artemis of the rows
of breasts like a sow and the bow
ready in her hand that kills and the herbs
that save in childbirth.

Ah, my name hung once like a can
on an ink stained girl blue as skim milk
lumpy with elbows, spiky with scruples,
who knelt in a tower raised of Shelley's bones
praying my demon lover asceticism
to grant one icy vision.

I found my body in the arms of lovers
and woke in the flesh alive, astounded
like a corpse sitting up in a judgment
day painting. My own five hound senses
turned on me, chased me, tore me
head from trunk. Thumb and liver
and jaw on the bloody hillside
twanged like frogs on the night I am alive!

A succession of lovers like a committee
of Congress in slow motion put me back

together, a thumb under my ear, the ear
in an armpit, the head sprouting feet.
Kaleidoscope where glass sparks pierced
my eyes, in love's funhouse I was hung
a mirror of flesh reflecting flaccid ideas
of men scouting their mothers through my womb,
a labyrinth of years in other
people's thoroughly furnished rooms.

I built myself like a house a poor family
puts up in the country: first the foundation
under a tarred flat roof like a dugout,
then the well in the spring and you get
electricity connected and maybe the next
fall you seal in two rooms and add some
plumbing but all the time you're living
there constructing your way out of a slum.
Yet for whom is this built if not to be shared
with the quick steps and low voice of love?

I cherish friendship and living that starts
in liking but the body is the church
where I praise and bless and am blessed.
My strength and my weakness are twins
in the same womb, mirrored dancers under
water, the dark and light side of the moon.
I know how truly my seasons have turned
cold and hot
around that lion-bodied sun.

Come step into the fire, come in,
come in, dance in the flames of the festival
of the strongest sun at the mountain top
of the year when the wheel starts down.
Dance through me as I through you.
Here in the heart of fire in the caves

of the ancient body we are aligned
with the stars wheeling, the midges swarming
in the humid air like a nebula, with the clams
who drink the tide and the heartwood clock
of the oak and the astronomical clock
in the blood thundering through the great heart
of the albatross. Our cells are burning
each a little furnace powered by the sun
and the moon pulls the sea of our blood.
This night the sun and moon dance
and you and I dance in the fire of which
we are the logs, the matches and the flames.

The sabbath of mutual respect

T I N N E

In the natural year come two thanksgivings,
the harvest of summer and the harvest of fall,
two times when we eat and drink and remember our dead
under the golden basin of the moon of plenty.

Abundance, Habondia, food for the winter,
too much now and survival later. After
the plant bears, it dies into seed.
The blowing grasses nourish us, wheat
and corn and rye, millet and rice, oat
and barley and buckwheat, all the serviceable
grasses of the pasture that the cow grazes,
the lamb, the horse, the goat; the grasses
that quicken into meat and cheese and milk,
the humble necessary mute vegetable bees,
the armies of the grasses waving their
golden banners of ripe seed.
                              The sensual
round fruit that gleams with the sun
stored in its sweetness.
                         The succulent
ephemera of the summer garden, bloodwarm
tomatoes, tender small squash, crisp
beans, the milky corn, the red peppers
exploding like cherry bombs in the mouth.

We praise abundance by eating of it,
reveling in choice on a table set with roses
and lilies and phlox, zucchini and lettuce
and eggplant before the long winter
of root crops.
               Fertility and choice:
every row dug in spring means weeks

of labor. Plant too much and the seedlings
choke in weeds as the warm rain soaks them.
The goddess of abundance Habondia is also
the spirit of labor and choice.
                           In another
life, dear sister, I too would bear six fat
children. In another life, my sister, I too
would love another woman and raise one child
together as if that pushed from both our wombs.
In another life, sister, I too would dwell
solitary and splendid as a lighthouse on the rocks
or be born to mate for life like the faithful goose.
Praise all our choices. Praise any woman
who chooses, and make safe her choice.

Habondia, Artemis, Cybele, Demeter, Ishtar,
Aphrodite, Au Set, Hecate, Themis, Lilith,
Thea, Gaia, Bridgit, The Great Grandmother of Us
All, Yemanja, Cerridwen, Freya, Corn Maiden,
Mawu, Amaterasu, Maires, Nut, Spider-Woman,
Neith, Au Zit, Hathor, Inanna, Shin Moo,
Diti, Arinna, Anath, Tiamat, Astoreth:
the names flesh out our histories, our choices,
our passions and what we will never embody
but pass by with respect. When I consecrate
my body in the temple of our history,
when I pledge myself to remain empty
and clear for the voices coming through
I do not choose for you or lessen your choice.

Habondia, the real abundance, is the power
to say yes and to say no, to open
and to close, to take or to leave

and not to be taken by force or law
or fear or poverty or hunger.
To bear children or not to bear by choice
is holy. To bear children unwanted
is to be used like a public sewer.
To be sterilized unchosen is to have
your heart cut out. To love women
is holy and holy is the free love of men
and precious to live taking whichever comes
and precious to live unmated as a peachtree.

Praise the lives you did not choose.
They will heal you, tell your story, fight
for you. You eat the bread of their labor.
You drink the wine of their joy. I tell you
after I went under the surgeon's knife
for the laparoscopy I felt like a trumpet
an Amazon was blowing sonorous charges on.
Then my womb learned to open on the full
moon without pain and my pleasure deepened
till my body shuddered like troubled water.
When my friend gave birth I held her in joy
as the child's head thrust from her vagina
like the sun rising at dawn wet and red.

Praise our choices, sisters, for each doorway
open to us was taken by squads of fighting
women who paid years of trouble and struggle,
who paid their wombs, their sleep, their lives
that we might walk through these gates upright.
Doorways are sacred to women for we
are the doorways of life and we must choose
what comes in and what goes out. Freedom
is our real abundance.

The perpetual migration

GORT

How do we know where we are going?
How do we know where we are headed
till we in fact or hope or hunch
arrive? You can only criticize,
the comfortable say, you don't know
what you want. Ah, but we do.

We have swung in the green verandas
of the jungle trees. We have squatted
on cloud-grey granite hillsides where
every leaf drips. We have crossed
badlands where the sun is sharp as flint.
We have paddled into the tall dark sea
in canoes. We always knew.

Peace, plenty, the gentle wallow
of intimacy, a bit of Saturday night
and not too much Monday morning,
a chance to choose, a change to grow,
the power to say no and yes, pretties
and dignity, an occasional jolt of truth.

The human brain, wrinkled slug, knows
like a computer, like a violinist, like
a bloodhound, like a frog. We remember
backwards a little and sometimes forwards,
but mostly we think in the ebbing circles
a rock makes on the water.

The salmon hurtling upstream seeks
the taste of the waters of its birth
but the seabird on its four-thousand-mile
trek follows charts mapped on its genes.
The brightness, the angle, the sighting

of the stars shines in the brain luring
till inner constellation matches outer.

The stark black rocks, the island beaches
of waveworn pebbles where it will winter
look right to it. Months after it set
forth it says, home at last, and settles.
Even the pigeon beating its short whistling
wings knows the magnetic tug of arrival.

In my spine a tidal clock tilts and drips
and the moon pulls blood from my womb.
Driven as a migrating falcon, I can be blown
off course yet if I turn back it feels
wrong. Navigating by chart and chance
and passion I will know the shape
of the mountains of freedom, I will know.

The longest night

The longest night is long drawn
as a freight blocking a grade crossing
in a prairie town when I am trying
to reach Kansas City to sleep and one
boxcar clatters after the other, after
and after in faded paint proclaiming
as they trundle through the headlights
names of 19th-century fortunes, scandals,
labor wars. Stalled between factory
and cemetery I lean on the cold wheel.
The factory is still, the machines
turned off; the cemetery looks boring
and factual as a parking lot. Too cold
for the dead to stir, tonight even
my own feel fragile as brown bags
carted to the dump. Ash stains the air.
Wheels of the freight clack by. Snow
hisses on the windshield of the rented car.
Always a storm at the winter solstice.

New moon, no moon, old moon dying,
moon that gives no light, stub
of a candle, dark lantern, face
without features, the zone of zero:
I feel the blood starting. Monthly
my womb opens on the full moon but
my body is off its rhythms. I am
jangled and raw. I do not celebrate
this blood seeping as from a wound.
I feel my weakness summoning me
like a bed of soft grey ashes
I might crawl into.

Here in the pit of the year scars overlap
scabs, the craters of the moon, stone
breaking stone. In the rearview mirror

my black hair fades into the night,
my cheeks look skeletal, my dark eyes,
holes a rat might hide in. I sense
death lurking up the road like a feral
dog abroad in the swirling snow.

Defeat, defeat, defeat, tedious
as modern headstones, regular as dentures.
My blood tastes salty as tears and rusty
as an old nail. Yet as I kick the car
over the icy tracks toward nowhere
I want to be, I am grinning. Lady, it's been
worse before, bad as the moon burning,
bad as the moon's horn goring my side,
that to give up now is a joke told
by the FBI minding the tap or the binoculars
staking me out on such a bitter night
when the blood slows and begins to freeze.
I grew up among these smoke-pitted houses
choking over the railroad between the factory
shuddering and the cemetery for the urban
poor, and I got out. They say that's
what you ask for. And how much more
I ask. To get everybody out.

Hecate, lady of the crossroads, vampires
of despair you loose and the twittering
bats of sleepless fear. The three-headed
dog barking in the snow obeys you.
Tonight I honor you, lady of last things.
Without you to goad me I would lie
late in the warm bed of the flesh.
The blood I coughed from my lungs that year
you stood at the foot of my bed was sour,

acrid, the taste of promises broken
and since then I have run twice as fast.
Your teeth are in me, like tiny headstones.
This moon is the void around which the serpent
with its tail in its mouth curls.
Where there is no color, no light,
no sound, what is? The dark of the mind.
In terror begins vision. In silence
I learn my song, here at the stone
nipple, the black moon bleeding,
the egg anonymous as water,
the night that goes on and on,
a tunnel through the earth.

Crescent moon like a canoe

FEARN

This month you carried me late and heavy
in your belly and finally near Tuesday
midnight you gave me light and life, the season
Kore returns to Demeter, and you suffer
and I cannot save you though I burn with dreams.

Memories the color of old blood,
scraps of velvet gowns, lace, chiffon veils,
your sister's stage costumes (Ziegfeld
didn't stint) we fingered together, you
padding in sneakers and wash-worn housedresses.

You grew celery by tucking sliced off
bottoms in the soil. You kept a compost
pile in 1940. Your tomatoes glowed
like traffic signals in the table-sized yard.
Don't kill spiders, you warned.

In an asbestos box in Detroit where sputtering
factories yellow the air, where sheets
on the line turn ashen, you nurtured
a backyard jungle. Every hungry cat
wanted to enter and every child.

You who had not been allowed to finish
tenth grade but sent to be a frightened
chambermaid, carried home every week
armloads of books from the library
rummaging them late at night, insomniac,

riffling the books like boxes of chocolates
searching for the candied cherries, the nuts,

hunting for the secrets, the formulae,
the knowledge those others learned
that made them shine and never ache.

You were taught to feel stupid; you
were made to feel dirty; you were
forced to feel helpless; you were trained
to feel lost, uprooted, terrified.
You could not love yourself or me.

Dreamer of fables that hid their own
endings, kitchen witch, reader of palms,
you gave me gifts and took them back
but the real ones boil in the blood
and swell in the breasts, furtive, strong.

You gave me hands that can pick up
a wild bird so that the bird relaxes,
turns and stares. I have handled
fifty stunned and injured birds and killed
only two through clumsiness, with your touch.

You taught me to see the scale on the bird
leg, the old woman's scalp pink as a rose
under the fluff, the golden flecks in the iris
of your eye, the silver underside of leaves
blown back. I am your poet, mother.

You did not want the daughter you got.
You wanted a girl to flirt as you did
and marry as you had and chew the same

sour coughed up cud, yet you wanted too
to birth a witch, a revenger, a sword

of hearts who would do all the things
you feared. Don't do it, they'll kill
you, you're bad, you said, slapping me down
hard but always you whispered, I could have!
Only rebellion flashes like lightning.

I wanted to take you with me, you don't
remember. We fought like snakes, biting
hard at each other's spine to snap free.
You burned my paper armor, rifled my diaries,
snuffed my panties looking for smudge of sex,

so I took off and never came back. You can't
imagine how I still long to save you,
to carry you off, who can't trust me
to make coffee, but your life and mine pass
in different centuries, under altered suns.

I see your blood soaking into the linoleum,
I see you twisted, a mop some giant hand
is wringing out. Pain in the careless joke
and shouted insult and knotted fist. Pain like knives
and forks set out on the domestic table.

You look to men for salvation and every year
finds you more helpless. Do I battle

for other women, myself included,
because I cannot give you anything
you want? I cannot midwife you free.

In my childhood bed we float, your sweet
husky voice singing about the crescent
moon, with two horns sharp and bright we would
climb into like a boat and row away
and see, you sang, where the pretty moon goes.

In the land where the moon hides, mothers
and daughters hold each other tenderly.
There is no male law at five o'clock.
Our sameness and our difference do not clash
metal on metal but we celebrate and learn.

My muse, your voice on the phone wavers with tears.
The life you gave me burns its acetylene
of buried anger, unused talents, rotted wishes,
the compost of discontent, flaring into words
strong for other women under your waning moon.

It breaks

You hand me a cup of water;
I drink it and thank you pretending
what I take into me so calmly
could not kill me. We take food
from strangers, from restaurants
behind whose swinging doors flies
swarm and settle, from estranged
lovers who dream over the salad plates
of breaking the bones of our backs
with a sledgehammer.

Trust flits through the apple
blossoms, a tiny spring warbler
in bright mating plumage. Trust
relies on learned pattern
and signal to let us walk down
stairs without thinking each
step, without stumbling.

I breathe smog and pollen
and perfume. I take parts
of your body inside me. I give you
the flimsy black lace and sweat
stained sleaze of my secrets.
I lay my sleeping body naked
at your side. Jump, you shout.
I do and you catch me.

In love we open wide as a house
to a summer afternoon, every shade up
and window cranked open and doors

flung back to the probing breeze.
If we love for long, we stand like row
houses with no outer walls
on the companionable side.

Suddenly we are naked,
abandoned. The plaster of bedrooms
hangs exposed to the street, wall
paper, pink and beige skins of broken
intimacy torn and flapping.

To fear you is fearing my left
hand cut off, a monstrous crab
scaling the slippery steps of night.
The body, the lineaments of old
desire remain, but the gestures
are new and harsh. Words unheard
before are spat out grating
with the rush of loosed anger.

Friends bear back to me banner
headlines of your rewriting of our
common past. You explain me away,
a dentist drilling a tooth.
I wonder at my own trust, how absolute
it was, mortal but part of me
like the bones of my pelvis.
You were the true center of my
cycles, the magnetic north
I used to plot my wanderings.

It is not that I will not love
again or give myself into partnership
or lie naked sweating secrets

like nectar, but I will never
share a joint checking account
and when some lover tells me, *Always,
baby,* I'll be thinking, sure,
until this one too meets an heiress
and ships out. After a bone breaks
you can see in X rays
the healing and the damage.

What's that smell in the kitchen?

All over America women are burning dinners.
It's lambchops in Peoria; it's haddock
in Providence; it's steak in Chicago
tofu delight in Big Sur; red
rice and beans in Dallas.
All over America women are burning
food they're supposed to bring with calico
smile on platters glittering like wax.
Anger sputters in her brainpan, confined
but spewing out missiles of hot fat.
Carbonized despair presses like a clinker
from a barbecue against the back of her eyes.
If she wants to grill anything, it's
her husband spitted over a slow fire.
If she wants to serve him anything
it's a dead rat with a bomb in its belly
ticking like the heart of an insomniac.
Her life is cooked and digested,
nothing but leftovers in Tupperware.
Look, she says, once I was roast duck
on your platter with parsley but now I am Spam.
Burning dinner is not incompetence but war.

Wind is the wall of the year

Much of what I had thought mine
essentially has fallen from me
of death, desertion, of ideas changed
conveniently as the temperature
drops and glaciers begin to creep.

The strong broad wind of autumn brushes
before it torn bags, seared apple skins,
moth wings, scraps of party velvet.
The hickory is a hard yellow scream
among maples' open raging mouths.

Lye in the wind eats the flesh from the land
till black skeletons arch against the sky,
till earth's great backbone rears, granite
picked clean of all abundance, consolation.
The road is strewn with broken ribs of branches.

Sparks spring up against the morning
devouring the last green, frying the sap.
A sheet of flame covers the day,
a cushion of haze in the bleeding afternoon,
a violent sunset over before supper.

I reach up into the sky and find
in ash of leaves, days and works, a love
I had expected to die still weaving,
dropping away to expose I must hope
some core to wait out this winter,

uncertain now if this is the winter
of my life or only a season like all
others to be entertained like a tyran-
nical guest or even enjoyed for the anatomy
it teaches as it rapidly dissects me.

Laocoön is the name
of the figure

That sweet sinewy green nymph
eddying in curves through the grasses:
she must stop and stare at him.
Of all the savage secret creatures
he imagines stealthy in the quivering
night, she must be made to approach,
she must be tamed to love him.
The power of his wanting will turn
her from hostile dark wandering
other beyond the circle of his
campfire into his own, his flesh,
his other wanting half. To keep her
she must be filled with his baby,
weighted down.
　　　　　　　Then suddenly
the horror of it: he awakens,
wrapped in the coils of the mother,
the great old serpent hag,
the hungry ravening witch who gives
birth and demands, and the lesser
mouths of the grinning children
gobbling his substance. He
must cut free.
　　　　　　An epic battle
in courts and beds and offices,
in barrooms and before the bar
and then free at last, he wanders.
There on the grassy hill, how the body
moves,
　　　　　her, the real one,
　　　　　　　　　　green
as a mayfly she hovers and he pounces.

Snow, snow

Like the sun on February ice dazzling;
like the sun licking the snow back
roughly so objects begin to poke through,
logs and steps, withered clumps of herb;
like the torch of the male cardinal
borne across the clearing from pine
to pine and then lighting among the bird
seed and bread scattered; like the sharp
shinned hawk gliding over the rabbit
colored marsh grass, exulting
in talon-hooked cries to his larger mate;
like the little pale green seedlings sticking
up their fragile heavy heads on white stalks
into the wide yellow lap of the pregnant sun;
like the sky of stained glass the eye seeks
for respite of the glitter that makes the lips
part; similar to all of these pleasures
of the failing winter and the as yet unbroken
blue egg of spring is our joy as we twist
and twine about each other in the bed
facing the window where the sun plays
the tabla of the thin cold air
and the snow sings soprano
and the emerging earth drones bass.

Digging in

This fall you will taste carrots
you planted, you thinned, you mulched,
you weeded and watered. You don't
know yet they will taste like yours,
not others, not mine.
This earth is yours as you love it.

We drink the water of this hill
and give our garbage to its soil.
We haul thatch for it and seaweed.
Out of it rise supper and roses
for the bedroom and herbs
for your next cold.

Your flesh grows out of this hill
like the maple trees. Its sweetness
is baked by this sun. Your eyes
have taken in sea and the light leaves
of the locust and the dark bristles
of the pine.

When we work in the garden you say
that now it feels sexual, the plants
pushing through us, the shivering
of the leaves. As we make love
later the oaks bend over us,
the hill listens.

The cats come and sit on the foot
of the bed to watch us.
Afterwards they purr.
The tomatoes grow faster and the beans.
You are learning to live in circles
as well as straight lines.

Let us gather at the river

I am the woman who sits by the river
river of tears
river of sewage
river of rainbows.
I sit by the river and count the corpses
floating by from the war upstream.
I sit by the river and watch the water
dwindle and the banks poke out like sore gums.
I watch the water change from green to shit brown.
I sit by the river and fish for your soul.
I want to lick it clean.
I want to turn it into a butterfly
that will weave drunkenly from orchid to rose.
I want to turn it into a pumpkin.
I want it to turn itself into a human being.

Oh, close your eyes tight and push hard
and evolve, altogether now. We can
do it if we try. Concentrate
and hold hands and push.
You can take your world back
if you want to. It's an araucana
egg, all blue and green
swaddled in filmy clouds.
Don't let them cook and gobble it,
azure and jungle green egg laid
by the extinct phoenix of the universe.

Send me your worn hacks of tired themes,
your dying horses of liberation,
your poor bony mules of freedom now.
I am the woman sitting by the river.
I mend old rebellions and patch them new.

Now the river turns from shit brown to bubbling blood
as an arm dressed in a uniform

floats by like an idling log.
Up too high to see, bombers big as bowling alleys
streak over and the automated battlefield
lights up like a Star Wars pinball machine.

I am the old woman sitting by the river scolding corpses.
I want to stare into the river and see the bottom
glinting like clean hair.
I want to outlive my usefulness
and sing water songs, songs
in praise of the green brown river
flowing clean through the blue green world.

The following is a list of the poems in this book and the dates they were written, which, as you can see, often is different from the date of the book publication.

From *BREAKING CAMP*

Kneeling at the pipes   1965
Visiting a dead man on a summer day   1966
Girl in white   1963
Noon of the sunbather   1961
A valley where I don't belong   1961
S. dead   1965
Hallow eve with spaces for ghosts   1965
Landed fish   1966
A few ashes for Sunday morning   1961
Concerning the mathematician   1966
Postcard from the garden   1964
The cats of Greece   1964
Sign   1967
A married walk in a hot place   1964
The Peaceable Kingdom   1966
Gasman invites the skyscrapers
    to dance   1967
The skyscrapers of the financial district
    dance with Gasman   1967
Breaking camp   1966, revised 1981

From *HARD LOVING*

Walking into love   1968
Community   1967
The neighbor   1966
The friend   1967
The morning half-life blues   began 1952,
    finished 1967
Erasure   1967
The cyclist   1966
Juan's twilight dance   1967
Learning experience   1966
Half past home   began 1960, finished 1968

Simple-song   1967
For Jeriann's hands   1967
I am a light you could read by   1967
Crabs   1968
Trajectory of the traveling Susan   1968
The butt of winter   1968
Bronchitis on the 14th floor   1968
The death of the small commune   1969
The track of the master builder   (published
    in *Hard Loving* as "Homo faber" 1967,
    rewritten 1981 for this vol.)
Why the soup tastes like the
    Daily News   1967
Curse of the earth magician on a
    metal land   1967

From *4-TELLING*

Letter to be disguised as a gas bill   1965
Sojourners   1966
Under the grind   1967
Somehow   1968
Never-never   1969
Ache's end   1969

From *TO BE OF USE*

A work of artiface   1970
What you waited for   1971
The secretary chant   1968
Night letter   1968
In the men's room(s)   1972
The nuisance   1968
I will not be your sickness   1968
The thrifty lover   1971
A shadow play for guilt   1969

297

Song of the fucked duck   1969
A just anger   1971
The crippling   1969
Right thinking man   1971
Barbie doll   1970
Hello up there   1972
High frequency   1973
The woman in the ordinary   1970
Unlearning to not speak   1971
Women's laughter   1972
Burying blues for Janis   1970
The best defense is offensive   began 1960,
   finished 1971
Icon   began 1960, finished 1972
Some collisions bring luck   1967
We become new   1971
Meetings like hungry beaks   1972
To be of use   1973
Bridging   1971
Doing it differently   1972
The spring offensive of the snail   1972
Councils   1971
Laying Down the Tower   1971–72

From *LIVING IN THE OPEN*

Living in the open   1974
I awoke with the room cold   1970
Gracious goodness   1971
Homesick   1973
Seedlings in the mail   1972
The daily life of the worker bee   1974
Cod summer   1972
A proposal for recycling wastes   1974
The bumpity road to mutual devotion   1974
On Castle Hill   1973
From *Sand Roads*   1975
Rough times   1972

Phyllis wounded   1975
Rape poem   1974
The consumer   1969
The provocation of the dream   1975
Looking at quilts   1974
To the pay toilet   1973
All clear   1972
Unclench yourself   1968
The homely war   1975

From *THE TWELVE-SPOKED WHEEL FLASHING*

The twelve-spoked wheel flashing   1976
What the owl sees   1975
The Greater Grand Rapids lover   1975
The Lansing bad penny come
   again blues   1975
The poet dreams of a nice warm motel   1976
Skimpy day at the solstice   1974
The market economy   1977
The love of lettuce   1977
Martha as the angel Gabriel   1976
Snow in May   1976
The window of the woman burning   1975
Going in   1975
Athena in the front lines   1962–75
The root canal   1976
Doors in the wind and the water   1976
You ask why sometimes I say stop   1977
Smalley Bar   1977
For Shoshana Rihn—Pat Swinton   1975
In the wet   1977
Crows   1975
If they come in the night   1977
At the core   1975
Beauty I would suffer for   1976
A gift of light   1977

A note about the author

Marge Piercy is the author of seven books of poetry: *Breaking Camp, Hard Loving, 4-Telling, To Be of Use, Living in the Open, The Twelve-Spoked Wheel Flashing, The Moon Is Always Female.* She has also published seven novels: *Going Down Fast, Dance the Eagle to Sleep, Small Changes, Woman on the Edge of Time, The High Cost of Living, Vida,* and *Braided Lives.* The University of Michigan's Arbor Press will be bringing out a volume of her essays, reviews, and interviews as part of the Poets on Poetry Series entitled *Parti-Colored Blocks for a Quilt.* She has also coauthored a play with Ira Wood, *The Last White Class.* She lives in Wellfleet, Massachusetts, with Ira Wood.

A note on the type

This book was set on the Linotype in Century Expanded, designed in 1894 by Linn Boyd Benton (1844–1932). Benton cut Century Expanded in response to Theodore De Vinne's request for an attractive, easy-to-read typeface to fit the narrow columns of his *Century Magazine.* Early in the nineteen hundreds Morris Fuller Benton updated and improved Century in several versions for his father's American Type Founders Company. Century remains the only American typeface cut before 1910 still widely in use today.

Composed by Maryland Linotype Composition Company, Baltimore, Maryland. Printed and bound by The Maple Press, York, Pennsylvania. Typography and binding design by Virginia Tan.